Politics of
Central Asia

Ram Rahul

Head, Department of Central Asian Studies,
Jawaharlal Nehru University,
New Delhi

BOOKS
10 East 53d St New York 10022
(a division of Harper & Row Publishers Inc.)

0737950

81735

VIKAS PUBLISHING HOUSE PVT LTD

5 DARYAGANJ, ANSARI ROAD, DELHI-110006
SAVOY CHAMBERS, 5 WALLACE STREET, BOMBAY-400001
10 FIRST MAIN ROAD, GANDHI NAGAR, BANGALORE-563009
80 CANNING ROAD, KANPUR-208001
17/19 HIGH STREET, HARLESDEN, LONDON, NW 10

Published in the U.S.A. 1974 by
HARPER & ROW PUBLISHERS, INC.
BARNES & NOBLE IMPORT DIVISION
ISBN 06-495776-4

Manufactured in The United States of America

Preface

Central Asia is one of the most fascinating areas of our world. The peoples of the area have made a profound contribution to the civilization of mankind. From Central Asia Buddhism travelled to China, Korea, and Japan. It helped to mould their distinctive civilizations. Again it was from Central Asia that science travelled to West Asia and thence to Europe. For about a millennium—i.e. from about the middle of the eighth century to the seventeenth— the Mongols and the Turks continuously maintained their political ascendancy in the region. Up to the end of the sixteenth century, Central Asia thus remained the seat of vast empires. Its subsequent decline was due to its incapability to share in the economic upsurge that the world elsewhere witnessed in the seventeenth, eighteenth, and nineteenth centuries. It was also barred by strong neighbours from outward expansion, for it no longer possessed sufficient strength for empire-building. The role of the Mongols in Sino-Russian relations remained vital even after the emergence of the imperial Manchus and Russia in Siberia and Central Asia. The role of the Turks in Anglo-Russian relations also remained vital even after the emergence of Britain and Russia in Khorasan and

Central Asia. The area of Central Asia is again growing in importance. It occupies a unique place both in the present relations of China, India, and the Union of Soviet Socialist Republics (USSR) and in Asian and international relations.

Since the establishment of the Central Asian republics of the Soviet Union in the 1920s, *Central Asia* has generally come to mean Soviet Central Asia. This image of Central Asia is not valid inasmuch as it excludes Afghanistan and Mongolia, which are nothing if not Central Asian. There is, moreover, Chinese Central Asia. The constant use and popularization of the term *Inner Asia* by American scholars instead of the term *Central Asia* for the entire area is mainly responsible for this narrowing down of the meaning of the expression *Central Asia* to denote only the Soviet part of the heartland of Asia. For the purpose of this study, I use the term *Central Asia* in its old, traditional sense. Indeed the organization of our Department of Central Asian Studies rests on this very basis. Incidentally, ours is the only University department on Central Asia in the world. According to our concept and definition, Central Asia comprises the entire area between the Great Wall of China in the east, the Himalaya, Hindu Kush, and Pamir Mountains in the south, the Caspian Sea and the Ural Mountains in the west, and Siberia in the north. Besides the peripheral areas of Manchuria, the Himalaya, the Caucasus, and Siberia, which are all important for the study of Central Asia, it consists of the two sovereign states of Afghanistan and the Mongolian People's Republic (MPR) and a large area each in China and the Soviet Union. Tibet, Sinkiang, and Inner Mongolia constitute Chinese Central Asia. Kazakstan and the Kirghiz, Tajik, Turkmen, and Uzbek republics constitute Soviet Central Asia.

This book deals only with certain aspects of the politics of Central Asia, not with their totality. I am concerned here chiefly with those aspects which constitute an important, though not basic, part of the politics of Central Asia. The boundaries of China, the frontiers of India, and the marches of Russia, in the context of the present border conflicts in Central Asia, are of the first importance from the viewpoint of the struggle for primacy there. The high priests of Buddhism and Islam have always played a great role in the politics as well as diplomacy of Central Asia. Although as religions Buddhism and Islam, which made a deep impact on the cultural traditions of Central Asia, do not play any role in the economy and politics of Central Asia any more, the lamas and mullahs are still important agents of change in Central Asia. They also matter in the peace movement and cultural diplomacy. All these aspects, and the history behind them, have a special bearing on the life and politics of Central Asia today.

The study concludes with a few observations on what the future might hold for Central Asia. These observations are based naturally on my understanding of the history and politics of Central Asia and on my assessment of Central Asia as a factor in the relations between China and the Soviet Union.

In the Appendixes I have included several documents important from the point of view of this study. Appendix I contains documents concluded by revolutionary Russia with the countries of Central Asia or with countries which have a bearing on Central Asia, whether historically or in contemporary politics. Appendix II contains documents concluded by revolutionary China with the countries of Central Asia or with countries which have a bearing on Central Asia, whether historically or in contemporary politics. In the Bibliography I have included books other than those mentioned in the footnotes. These books, though not concerned with Central Asian politics as such, are nevertheless useful as background material for the study and understanding of the politics of the region.

I take this opportunity to express my thanks to Girja Kumar, Librarian, Jawaharlal Nehru University (New Delhi), Arthur Lall, Professor of International Affairs at Columbia University (New York City), K.L. Mehta, India's Ambassador to Afghanistan (Kabul), S.N. Prasad, Director of National Archives of India, (New Delhi), S.K. Roy, India's Ambassador to Mexico (Mexico City), and N.K. Rustomji, Chief Secretary of Meghalaya (Shillong), for their interest in my programme of explorations in Central Asia.

Ram Rahul

Contents

ONE

Introduction

By and large the neighbouring countries of China, India, and Russia or the Powers based there have had a deep impact on the politics of Central Asia. Central Asia was one of the key areas of rivalry for supremacy between Britain and Russia through most of the nineteenth century, and between Japan and the Soviet Union in the first half of the twentieth. Just as the coming together of Afghanistan, Iran, and Turkey and the Sovietization of Russian Central Asia in the 1920s were matters of grave concern to the makers of the British policy towards Central Asia, the emergence of Japan in China and in the Chinese territories bordering the Soviet Union in the 1930s caused much anxiety in the Soviet Union. Japanese supremacy in Manchuria and Soviet supremacy in Sinkiang was indicative of a kind of balance of power in Central Asia. Japanese expansion in China threatened the Soviet position not only in northern Manchuria, western Inner Mongolia, Sinkiang, and Outer Mongolia, but also in the Soviet Far East and Siberia. Central Asia is now an area of a struggle for primacy between China and the Soviet Union. This chapter deals with these different phases of the politics of Central Asia by way of a background to the chapters that follow.

Russia advanced towards Turkey and Persia during the early part of the eighteenth century. This advance, especially its campaign of 1826-28 against Persia, put it in conflict with Britain.   In formulating its policy towards Persia and Central Asia, therefore, Russia found it necessary to take the British interest there into account. Similarly Britain had to take due note of the Russian interest in Persia and Central Asia.   Britain and Russia became deeply involved in the area.   Their advance was not for commercial purposes alone: it was conquest plus commerce, commerce consisting in the sale of just their goods and in the exclusion of those of other nations.   The local Powers realized this and also the growing antagonism between the two expanding Powers.   Britain and Russia confronted each other from China to Persia in the 1880s and the 1890s.   The position of Afghanistan and Persia in relation to the defence of India was of vital importance to Britain.   The moves made by Britain in Afghanistan and Persia, as well as in Tibet, roused Russian suspicions of British designs.   About the turn of the century Russia's position in Central Asia conferred on it special advantages *vis-a-vis* Britain and China.

Afghanistan, which achieved freedom from Mughal and Persian imperialisms in 1747, inadvertently became involved in the "game" of the British and Russian power politics in Central Asia.   (In 1762, in response to an appeal from the chiefs of the Kazak tribes and from the ruler of Kokand for help against the expedition of Ch'ieng-lung— later Emperor Ch'ieng-lung, *r.* 1792-1810—who had threatened to attack Samarkand and Tashkent, powerful Ahmad Shah Abdali, *r.* 1747-73, sent a force to the defence of Tashkent.   In 1921, powerful Amanullah, *r.* 1919-29, supported the Basmachis and the forces of Bukhara against the Bolsheviks.)   Besides the pressures and pulls of the British and Russian empires expanding in Central Asia, Afghanistan was handicapped by internal turmoil, with one group after another contending to seize power.   Both the internal instability and the Anglo-Russian struggle for ascendancy in Central Asia eventually forced upon it the position not merely of a buffer, but of a protectorate—of a state prohibited from conducting its own foreign relations with any Power other than Britain.

The British advanced steadily and irresistibly towards Afghanistan and Persia, and the Russians advanced as steadily and irresistibly beyond the Caspian Sea, and each felt annoyed at the other's getting in its way.   The British, ever jealous of their vast possessions in the East, feared that the real objective behind the Russian thrust was to deprive them of their possessions in India.   They never liked the idea of the Russian Government to become a party to the question of Afghanistan; for they wanted Afghanistan to preserve its integrity at all costs. The Russians, on the other hand, feared that under British influence Afghanistan might become a disturbing factor in the peace of Central Asia. In 1869, therefore, the two Powers— Britain and Russia—began negotiations on the status of Afghanistan. In January 1873, they concluded an agreement in St Petersburg concerning the northern limits of Afghanistan. By the agreement of 1873 Russia also gave a positive commitment that Afghanistan lay wholly outside its sphere of influence. By the Anglo-Russian Convention of 31 August 1907 the two further defined their respective spheres of influence in Persia, Afghanistan, and Tibet. By the compact of 1907, Britain undertook not to annex or occupy any part of Afghanistan, and Russia confirmed that Afghanistan lay outside its sphere of influence. Thus, the negotiations which began with the aim of creating a buffer state ended up in the carving out of spheres of influence.

Britain and Russia, which had both evinced special interest in Eastern Turkistan ever since the first half of the nineteenth century, pursued an active forward policy there from the 1860s onwards. Their interest in Eastern Turkistan (now called Sinkiang) in the 1870s, in fact, represented their recognition of its independence from China. During the decline of the Chinese Empire, British and Russian imperialisms competed with each other to gain strategic control over it. The Chinese, like the Afghans, withdrew from much of the Pamir region. Later, after the mid 1880s, the British developed a policy of appeasement of China all along India's northern frontiers. They pressurized the ruler of Jammu and Kashmir into withdrawing from the trans-Karakoram and especially to waive Hunza's claim to its pastures in the Pamir region. After the Russian Revolution the British concerted their efforts to stop the spread of Soviet influence in Sinkiang. However, in the early 1930s, Sinkiang fell into the economic orbit of the Soviet Union. In the mid 1930s the Soviet Union pursued certain politico-military objectives in Sinkiang, and Sinkiang became practically an outpost of the Soviet Union.

The spread of Soviet influence in Sinkiang had dimensions which the British Government in India could not afford to ignore. The State of Jammu and Kashmir with its vast Muslim population was contiguous to the Soviet Union. During 1936-40 the Chinese administration in Sinkiang constructed posts, and held them in strength, on the Hunza border facing the approaches to India. In the early 1940s thousands of Indians, mostly Muslims from Kashmir, who were engaged in the caravan trade with Central Asia and who had been living in Yarkand, Khotan, and Kashgar for generations, had to throw away their British Indian passports because the Chinese regime frowned upon those not adopting Chinese nationality. All trade between Sinkiang and India ceased. The Japanese agents also spread the rumour that the Soviet Union was trying to gain a foothold in Tibet. The British Government in India, already uneasy over the developments in Tibet, suspected that the pro-Chinese elements in Lhasa might well be the puppets of Japan. It was not wrong; for Japanese Buddhist monks and trade agents were pouring into the land to spread Japanese influence. Indeed Japan was playing a more active game than the British suspected.

The Soviet Union was forced to divert all its attention and energy to its war with Germany, which began in the summer of 1941. It, therefore, entered into an agreement with China towards the end of 1942 which empowered the latter to take over regular control of Sinkiang. This proved favourable to the British; for the Chinese relaxed their restrictions on the Hunza border and instead strengthened their posts on the Sarikol border with the Soviet Union. They also stopped harassing travellers on the route to India. There were also other signs of improved relations between the British and the Chinese in Sinkiang. For instance, the Chinese allowed the opening of a British consulate at Urumchi (formerly Tihwa) and a postal service between India and Sinkiang for the first time.

The Chinese-Communists "liberated" Sinkiang in October 1949, and made it an integral part of their unitary state—that is, the People's Republic of China. On 1 October 1955, the Chinese Government reorganized Sinkiang as the Sinkiang-Uigur Autonomous Region of the People's Republic of China. Sinkiang was caught up in the movement for autonomy during the brief "Hundred Flowers" period in 1957. Ever since it has remained restless under Chinese rule and reign of terror. Much uneasiness now obtains in the relations between the Chinese Government and the people of the Sinkiang-Uigur Autonomous Region.

The "liberation" of Sinkiang is of great significance in the history of India's connection with Central Asia; for, after occupying Sinkiang, the Chinese Communists refused to acknowledge the diplomatic status of R.D. Sathe, who was then India's Consul-General in Kashgar in south-western Sinkiang bordering Tibet, India, Afghanistan, and the Soviet Union. (He was the only Indian to hold that post.) They did not like a "foreign" post in this remote and strategic part of their country. They were not sure if India was fully sovereign and independent as yet. Perhaps they were also not clear as to the intentions or policy of the Government of India towards Central Asia. They suspected that India might serve as the watch-man of the interests of other Powers. It is quite clear that the Government of India had not fully explained to China the nature of the political change in the country on 15 August 1947. China then was not suspicious of any design on the part of the Soviet Union, a fraternal socialist Power. Eventually Sathe withdrew to New Delhi via Ladakh, completing a circle as it were; for he had travelled to Kashgar via Chungking and Urumchi in 1948. The Government of India could not take any retaliatory action as China, imperialist or nationalist or revolutionary, had never had any consular establishment in the region of Jammu and Kashmir. Perhaps the Government of India was not willing to accord reciprocal consular rights to the People's Republic of China in Leh or Srinagar for fear that such a step on its part might enable the Chinese to spread their influence in the Western Himalaya and Tibet. Clearly this was a case of missed oportunity. The Chinese consular presence in Leh or Srinagar would have meant the Chinese acceptance of the State of Jammu and Kashmir as a part of India. It is possible that the Chinese Government had already made up its mind on the question of the political status of Jammu and Kashmir, and might have spurned the suggestion of the Indian Government to station consular personnel in Leh or Srinagar in exchange for the stationing of Indian consular personnel in Kashgar. However, the recall of Sathe from Kashgar marked the first step in India's withdrawal from Central Asia.

The Tibetans, who suspected the British of evil designs on their country, resented British influence in the Himalaya. They felt that it was directed essentially against their country. The British were originally interested in the Himalaya, as in Central Asia, in expanding their trade in Tibet, as well as in China. When, however, they heard rumours of Russian influence in the counsels of Lhasa and noted China's inability to prevent acts of aggression by the Tibetans on the border countries of Garhwal and Sikkim during 1880-1900, they subordinated their interest in trade to the security of their Indian

Empire.   Their main preoccupation in the Himalaya and Tibet thus became one of containing Russian influence there.   They did not relax their vigil even when the Russians were at war with Japan over the question of Korea; for, by 1895 the Chinese game of duplicity had been exposed.   China had always enjoyed sufficient influence in Tibet though little power and its failure to restrain Tibet, therefore, irked the British, who sent a military expedition to Tibet in 1903-4. This expedition disturbed the easy pattern of the Chinese suzerainty over Tibet.   The growth of British influence in Tibet also sharpened Nepalese jealousy and reduced the importance and prestige of the Nepalese agent in Lhasa, sole intermediary between Tibet and the outside world.   It also increased Russian suspicion of British imperial policy.

It was in this context that Britain and Russia negotiated the Anglo-Russian Convention of 31 August 1907.   The convention defined the British and Russian spheres of influence in Central Asia and spelt out the specific understanding that the two Powers should deal with Tibet only through the agency of China.   This greatly buttressed the Chinese position in Tibet.   Though the British outwardly maintained that there was no substance in the Chinese claim of authority over Tibet, they pursued a policy of appeasement towards China.   By their acknowledgement of China's suzerainty over Tibet, they made the chances of an understanding with the Tibetans all but impossible. The Chinese, on their part, regarded British penetration into Tibet in 1903-4 as encroachment in a sphere historically their own.   In 1908 they appointed Chao Erh feng, who, as Warden of the Marches of Eastern Tibet, had annexed several frontier States in Eastern Tibet in 1905, as *Amban* (Political Agent) in Lhasa and charged him with the task of reconsolidating Chinese control over Tibet.   The main aim of the Chinese forward policy in Tibet during 1910-11 was to reduce it to the position of a Province of China.

The rise of the Chinese power in Tibet in the wake of the British expedition to Tibet brought Nepal and Tibet closer, each to the other, although an appeal by Tibet for help, in terms of the Nepalese-Tibetan Peace Treaty of 1856, did not produce results.   Nepal was greatly perturbed by the Chinese moves to abridge its special rights in Tibet, and to reduce it to the position of a vassal in terms of the Sino-Nepalese settlement of 1792.

The Tibetans expelled the Chinese from Lhasa, and Tibet, in 1912. The growing spirit of independence in Lhasa also led to renewed resentment of Nepal's position of privilege in the country. Under the Nepalese-Tibetan Treaty of 1856, Nepalese nationals trading with Tibet or living there were exempt from payment of duties or taxes of any kind, even though the Tibetans enjoyed no such exemption in Nepal. The Nepalese residing in Tibet could marry Tibetan women, but the treaty granted no such right to the Tibetans residing in Nepal to marry Nepalese women. Boys born of Nepalese-Tibetan parents were always regarded as Nepalese whereas girls of such parentage were always regarded as Tibetan. Tibetan laws governing the catching of fish, collecting of honey, hunting or smoking did not apply to Nepalese offenders. The Nepalese representative in Lhasa, appointed to look after Nepalese trade affairs in Tibet and particularly the relations between Nepalese traders there and the Tibetan Government and traders, exercised jurisdiction over all the Nepalese in Tibet and claimed it over Nepalese-Tibetan half-breeds as well. The Tibetan Government particularly resented the presence of the Nepalese agents in Gyantse and Shigatse, who seem to have been appointed between 1902 and 1904.

Nepal's special position in Tibet continued untill 1 August 1955, when the People's Republic of China and Nepal normalized their relations. Nepal did not automatically accept the change in the political status of Tibet vide the Sino-Tibetan agreement of 23 May 1951. Nor did it agree that the change in the political status of Tibet affected in any way the special economic and political relations between Nepal and Tibet. However in spite of friction and misunderstanding on several counts, Nepal's relations with new China were not unfriendly. The settlement between China and Tibet in 1951 had immediate repercussions on the advantages which Nepal enjoyed in Tibet. This was very irking to General Chang-Chingwu, Peking's highest representative in Lhasa; for it suggested a position of Nepalese supremacy in Tibet, and such a situation was unacceptable to China, which wanted immediate cancellation or repudiation of the Nepalese-Tibetan Treaty of 1856, however determined Nepal might be to retain its advantageous position in Tibet. In the light of its experience of a similar situation in 1905-11, Nepal thought it best to normalize its relations with China instead of striving with a strong and united China. Eventually, by the Sino-Nepalese agreement of 20 September 1956, Nepal accepted the principle of China's sovereignty over Tibet and relinquished its special position in Tibet.

As for the British Government in India, it recognized China's suzerainty over Tibet, but not its sovereignty, when the Republic of China, established on 1 January 1912, claimed Tibet, and objected to its right actively to intervene in Tibet's internal affairs. In the context of the question of the recognition of the Republic of China muted by the United States in the spring of 1913. both the British and Russian Governments insisted on prior recognition by the Chinese of their respective interests in Tibet and Mongolia. In a memorandum on 17 August 1913 the British Government plainly declared that until China accepted its demand, it would not recognize the Republic. It took this hard line because the Tibetans had them-selves eliminated Chinese influence from their country in 1912 and had established a connection with Russia through Mongolia in 1913. Russia also had strengthened its hold on Mongolia and was drawing nearer to Tibet. When Tibet concluded a treaty of alliance with Mongolia, which was virtually under Russia's protection, in Urga on 11 January 1913, Russia acquired a special though indirect position in Tibet.

The British finally succeeded in getting China's consent for the maintenance of the *status quo* in Tibet, and for the holding of a confe-rence of the representatives of the British, Chinese, and Tibetan Governments to define the political status of Tibet. The conference, convened in Simla in 1913, broke down on the question of the frontier between China and Tibet. China never ratified the convention drawn up and initialled by the conference. Nevertheless, Yuan Shih-kai, Provisional President of the Republic of China since 12 February 1912, took full advantage of the tentative agreement. He announced China's recognition of the autonomy of Outer Tibet and Outer Mongolia on 7 October 1913; and on the same day the British and Russian Governments recognized China.

The Simla Conference, however, resulted in an agreement between the British and Tibetan Governments on the frontier between Assam and Tibet from Bhutan to Burma. This agreement on the frontier, which came almost as a *quid pro quo* from Tibet to the British for their help in the settlement of matters then in dispute between China and Tibet, was not the prime objective of the conference. The British wanted such an agreement not so much because they needed it to check Tibetan activity in their territories south of the main ridge of the Eastern Himalaya as because they knew that behind Tibet, and ready to absorb it at the first opportunity, lay China, which in its expan-sionist period before 1912 had established posts in several places within the Assam frontier with Tibet.

The British Government in India obviously realized that China wanted both to dominate Tibet and to incorporate as much of that country as possible, but lacked the power to do so. British policy, therefore, was geared to ensure the survival of an autonomous, secluded, and friendly Tibet on India's 2,000-mile-long frontier. To that end it sought an agreement with China and/or Tibet that would secure Tibet's frontiers and constitute a definite barrier to China's advance towards India. These considerations are thus the *raison d'etre* of the formula of Outer Tibet (under Chinese suzerainty) and Inner Tibet (under a measure of Chinese rule) announced in 1914.

The British sent a communication on 26 August 1921 to the Chinese Government, reminding it of the nature of their interest in Tibet and restating their policy of maintaining the integrity of Tibet and of ensuring in Tibet a Government capable of keeping peace and order along India's frontiers. They sent representatives to Tibet to obtain first-hand information about events on the Sino-Tibetan frontier, as well as to demonstrate to the Chinese that they were in earnest about reopening the abortive negotiations of 1913-14. Further, they advised the Government of Tibet to build up its army, for they felt that in the event of negotiations China was unlikely to talk on a basis of equality and reason with a weak Tibet.

Despite the expulsion of Chinese troops in 1912 the Government of Tibet and its friends were well aware that the Chinese had not left for ever and that as soon as they were in a position to do so, they would come back. Tibet had never been able to prevent the Chinese from returning whenever the latter had made a determined effort to do so under a strong Central Government. Dalai Lama XIII (1874-1933), who was grateful to the British Government for according him asylum in 1910 and helping him greatly during his asylum in India in 1910-12, was well aware of it. The Tibetan Government, therefore, took the advice of the British seriously. It decided to strengthen the army and to give Western training to its military personnel and selected several senior officers for training in India. Indeed it was so anxious to be on even terms with China that in the 1920s it imported considerable quantities of arms and ammunition from the Japanese to supplement what it had obtained from the British.

Tibet, whose frontiers march along China, Burma, India, and Nepal, needed a large army. According to the old system, the responsibility for collecting soldiers to meet any military threat was that of the landlords. An army consisting of untrained men hurrie‹ recruited could hardly hope to hold its ground against Chin‹ trained army. Thus Tibet had need to strengthen and train its arn The stumbling-block was want of adequate funds The en‹ country was already cut up into estates, big and small, the big‹ ones being property of Tibet's leading monasteries. When ‹ Government asked the monasteries for contributions, the‹ said t‹ they did not have enough money even for religious purposes and the expenses of the monks. When the Government reminded administration of the Tashilhunpo Monastery to expedite paym‹ of the levy, the Panchhen Lama, as its head, only explained his pr‹ lems. When more pressure was put on the monasteries, they thou that all this was due to the influence of the British. This increa the misunderstanding between them and the Government of Lh‹ The Panchhen Lama felt that the levy had made his position untena and fled secretly northwards in the winter of 1923. (He died Jyekundo along the Sino-Tibetan frontier in 1937.) Thus the Bri‹ position in Tibet suffered a setback. Dalai Lama XIII wiel‹ enormous power, and he realized fully the need for adequate milit preparations for the defence of Tibet. However, he was not abl‹ do much in the direction of army reform. It was this failure wh eventually became responsible for the reappearance of China in Ti in 1950-51.

Notwithstanding this misunderstanding of their motives in Ti and elsewhere, the British were able to exercise a measure of con‹ over the military situation in Central Asia. By supplying arms to Tibetans, they checked the growing Japanese influence in Tibet ‹ Central Asia. They could hardly afford to regard with equanim the rise of a rival Power like Japan.

After 1930, China vigorously endeavoured to reassert its old p‹ tion in Tibet. Till 1945, however, it camouflaged its moves so as ‹ to offend Britain, for it depended on Britain for munitions for war against Japan. The main problem before British diplomacy ‹ to determine whether the dominating Power in Tibet was going be a strong and united China or a China dominated by Japan or ‹ Soviet Union, and whether China's policy towards Tibet was on‹ (1) penetration, (2) forward policy, or (3) incorporation of Tibet China. Though preoccupied with Japan, China devoted consi rable attention and energy to forming a new Province, Sikang, ‹ of Kham and the ethnically Tibetan western part of Szechwan.

was the Chinese Communists and the Japanese who, by pressing the Kuomintang hard, prevented it from getting any time to make a strong move against Tibet. Tibetan sympathies were, therefore, always with Japan, both because Japan was a Buddhist country and because Japan was able to stop China from invading Tibet.

The British could achieve their objective of keeping Tibet as an adequate buffer for the entire frontier of India with the help primarily of the Tibetans themselves. They, therefore, extended to them their diplomatic support in China and helped them in various ways. The Tibetans on their part fully realized that the British in their own interest were trying to maintain the essential integrity of their country. This knowledge constituted a strong political bond between the British and the Tibetans.

When independence came to India on 15 August 1947, the Government of free India inherited this British position in Tibet along with all British rights and oligations under the conventions of 1904 and 1914. While it sought friendly relations with China, it revised all the old treaties with Bhutan, Sikkim, and Nepal in order to forestall any serious misunderstanding between them and Tibet, as also between them and itself. The claims made by China in the past to certain areas in India's borderlands with cultural and ethnic associations with Tibet had alerted it in this regard.

In 1950, India expressed its determination to retain its special rights in Tibet. On the eve of the Chinese advance into Tibet in the winter of 1950, India expressed its disappointment with China's using force in solving its dispute. China ignored India's recommendation of peaceful methods. In fact, it rebuked India for trying to frustrate through diplomacy its desire to "liberate" Tibet. India did not do anything more than protest. This marked a departure in India's policy towards Tibet. On 15 September 1952, the Government of India converted its mission in Lhasa into a consulate-general under the jurisdiction of its embassy in Peking. This change marked the end of the political co-operation between India and Tibet on a basis of equality. It also marked India's unequivocal acknowledgement of China's supremacy in Tibet. The signing of an agreement by China and India on "Trade and Intercourse between the Tibet Region of China and India" in Peking on 27 April 1954, which put the seal of formality on India's acceptance of Tibet as an integral part of China, completed the process of India's withdrawal from Central Asia, a process it initiated in 1949-50 by recalling its Consul General from

Kashgar.   This was the begining of a new phase.

China was jubilant at the conclusion of the agreement of 1954 for it had secured recognition from India that Tibet was an integra part of Chinese territory.   It had also effectively put an end to India special position there.   India had acquiesced in China's ultima control of Tibetan relations and had denied itself the right to interfer in Tibetan affairs.

The debates on the inscription of the question of Tibet on the agend of the General Assembly of the United Nations in the wake of the up rising of Tibet on 10 March 1959 and the draft resolution calling upo the Chinese to restore to the Tibetans their freedom and fundamenta rights in 1960 provided an interesting picture of the changing inter national attitude to Tibet.   The attitudes of Britain and Japan—tw countries which have paid special attention to Central Asia in moder times—reflected more than a line-up of bloc alignment.   China whose anti-British bias always led it to underestimate the desire c the Tibetans for freedom from Chinese overlordship, ascribed tha desire to Indian machinations.   The Soviet Union, historical Britain's chief rival for ascendancy in Tibet, regarded the situatio there as entirely an internal affair of China.   The United State which had always treated Tibet as an integral part of China, quietl suggested its dismemberment from China.   The most importar development was the acceptance of Tibet as a part of China by Asia major countries, particularly by Indonesia, which had only recentl freed itself from foreign rule.

Historians dispute China's claim to Tibet.   China held sway ove Tibet as over Mongolia, but its suzerainty over Mongolia was reduce to non-existence by Russia in the early 1920s.   Mongolia, therefor escapes "liberation" by China.   Or does it?   However, like th Mongols, the Tibetans also looked for help powerful enough to giv them the chance to shape their own destiny.

On the fall of the Manchu regime in China in 1911, the Jetsundamb Khutukhtu, the religious head and leader of the Mongols, declare Mongolia's freedom and independence from Chinese control an overlordship.   In order to establish itself as the paramount Power- a Power superior to the British and the Japanese—Russia too advantage of this event to advance into China's sphere of influenc bring Mongolia within its own sphere of influence, and grant it pro tection.   Naturally the Mongols, who had suffered Chinese domina tion for long, accepted the Russian assurance of protection of thei independence. Mongolia is now under the protection of the Soviet State, successor to the Russian State.

The torch of the Russian Revolution—the torch of freedom—also shed its light on the Mongols and inspired them to fight for complete independence from Chinese rule. The formation of an independent People's Government of Mongolia on 10 July 1921 marked the victory of the people's revolution. The First People's Great Assembly, which adopted a constitution on 26 November 1924, proclaimed the birth of the Mongolian People's Republic (MPR) and renamed Urga—the capital of the country—*Ulan Bator* (Red Hero). A plebiscite, held on 20 October 1945, overwhelmingly favoured the independence and separation of the MPR. In January 1946, China formally recognized the independence of the MPR. The Sino-Soviet Treaty of 14 February 1950 confirmed and guaranteed it.

The Mongols hailed the revolution in China as a "true Asian revolution". Mongol intellectuals and the People's Revolutionary Party felt much sympathy and admiration for revolutionary China, and not a few believed that given the choice Mongolia would befriend China rather than the Soviet Union. This was a passing phase. It is now many years since every hint of pro-Chinese sentiment disappeared from all of Mongolia. In place of praise for their Chinese friends and thanks for their help the Mongols now point to the efforts made by China—with specific mention of each such effort—to subert their regime, to commit acts of harassment and treachery against their Government, to humiliate the people. They, therefore, staunchly support the Soviet Union today in its policy towards the Sino-Indian border dispute, the West Asian crisis, Vietnam, and so on. They think the Soviet policy to be right. Pro-Sovietism, therefore, is a conscious decision of the Mongols. China pressurizes them to accept its point of view. The Mongols, who want to be masters of their own house and to be free to decide their own destiny, consider the Chinese advice as a piece of interference in their affairs and strongly resent it. The basic factor determining and governing the Mongolian alliance with the Soviet Union is, therefore, the Mongol anxiety over Chinese intentions towards their country. They know of the Chinese attempts to colonize Inner Mongolia.

If China's history points to anything, it is this: China's main concern has always been with itself and with the cultural superiority of the Chinese people over all others. To them, the people on their periphery have always been barbarians. Chinese officials know how to create an atmosphere of superiority and power without any great display of force, and to impress upon simple-minded border people the dignity of their country and the excellence of their civilization. In the case of the Mongols, these impressions are particularly marked strongly, as they have adopted many features of the Chinese civilization in their life and culture.

Long centuries ago the Russian objective in Central Asia was to unify all subjects of the Tsar in a single allegiance to the State Church. The fear that the Muslims might be attracted to the Ottoman Empire was an additional factor in the Russian advance. Later, after the Revolution of 1917, the Soviet Union hoped to influence Afghanistan, Iran, and Turkey through granting federal autonomy to Uzbekistan, Turkmenistan, Azerbaijan, and finally Tajikstan. When, however, it realized in the early 1930s that pan-Turkic and pan-Iranian influences might foster secessionist tendencies, it came down heavily on Islam and reduced the federal autonomy of the Muslim nationalities in Soviet Central Asia and the Caucasus to a mere administrative formality. It would be interesting to know, in the context of the present relationship between China and the Soviet Union, the nature of Soviet policy towards such Muslim areas as the area inhabited by the Kazaks, who live on both sides of the Sino-Soviet frontier in Central Asia.

In the nineteenth century, Turkey, Iran, and Afghanistan suspected Russia and its objectives towards them. They thought that Russia wanted to absorb them or draw them to itself or, failing to do that, divide them between Britain and itself. Now they not only have good relations with the Soviet Union but are eager to develop special neighbourly relationship with it. The Mongols have always played an important role in the relations between their two great neighbours. In the past the Russians had to pass through Mongolia on their way to China. (The Mongol tribes lay between the two empires of China and Russia.) It is interesting to note that the Khalkha Mongols, who were bitterly opposed to Russia during the Sino-Russian negotiations over the Amur territories at Nerchhinsk in 1689, are now acting as friends of the Soviet Union.

Recently there have been spectacular developments in Central Asia like the Sino-Indian conflict of 1962 and Sino-Soviet border conflict of 1969. China has advanced its claim to certain Indian territories south of the Himalaya and to certain Soviet territories both east and west of Lake Baikal. Besides, there are also disputes over border pasture and trade. For centuries, thousands of Afghan nomads have been accustomed to wintering in the neighbouring countries. Similarly, owing to strained Sino-Soviet and Sino-Indian relations, the border trade of Sinkiang and Tibet has been seriously affected. Many of the disputes and problems of the countries of Central Asia are interconnected. For the solution of each individual dispute, unconditional bilateral talks are desirable. Of course, none of the disputes is strictly bilateral in scope. For various reasons all these disputes are now internationalized.

China's irredentism is in line with its view, held consistently throughout history, that, regardless of inconvenient treaty provisions, China has the moral right to claim any territory that had at any time been a part of its empire. Treaties that might work to the disadvantage of China were "unequal" and *ipso facto* illegal. It follows that any territory, once in Chinese hands, must forever remain in Chinese hands and, if lost, must be reclaimed and regained at the first opportunity. China does not regard any loss of territory on its part anywhere as legal or valid. Such a loss would at best denote just a passing weakness. The Soviet Government has succeeded in taking the issue from the field of battle to the sphere of diplomacy. Let us see what will happen; for the outcome of the Sino-Soviet negotiations will have a special bearing not only on the politics of Central Asia, but also on Asian and world politics.

TWO

Boundaries of China

China's questioning the validity of its boundary with India and of India's title to large parts of Arunachal Pradesh and Ladakh has resulted in deep misunderstanding and bitter conflict between the two countries. However, a study of the making and development of China's boundaries with countries other than India, Bhutan, and Sikkim in the periods of the Manchu Empire (1644-1911), the Republic of China (1911-1949), and the People's Republic (1949-   ) would show that the international boundaries inherited by the People's Republic are generally in accordance with custom, tradition, and the principles of geography established long before the advent of Western imperialism in China or Asia, although China's approach to the settling of such border disputes as have arisen in the course of history has varied according to the circumstances of different situations.

Owing to China's first boundary settlement with Russia as long ago as the seventeenth century, this chapter approaches the subject of China's boundaries from the Russian side. It excludes from its purview any appraisal of the nature and position of China's boundaries with Hong Kong and Macao, which are the furthest possessions of Britain and Portugal respectively in the extreme east and which China regards as territories falling within its legitimate boundaries. Indeed the Government of China may take such measures as it may deem fit to seize them when it feels that the conditions are ripe enough for such an action.

USSR SECTOR

The 4,500-mile boundary between China and the USSR, the world's longest frontier, stretching from the Sea of Japan in the east to the Pamir mountains in the west, separates the Chinese frontier provinces of Kirin and Heilungkiang (formerly Sunkiang) and the Inner Mongolian Autonomous Region (Chahar, Suiyuan, Ninghsia, and Kansu before the administrative organization of 19 June 1954) and the frontier parts of south-eastern Siberia in the eastern section and the Sinkiang—Uigur Autonomous Region (Sinkiang from 1878 to 1954) and the Kazakh, Kirghiz, and Tajik republics of the Soviet Union in the western section. The Mongolian People's Republic (MPR) intervenes in the central section.

Russia's eastward drive in the seventeenth century brought it into close contact and conflict with China. By the 1640s Russia had reached both the Amur River, the 1,500-mile boundary with northeast China, and the Pacific Ocean. Shun-chin (r. 1644-62), the first Manchu Emperor, regarded the Amur territories as the hunting and pasture lands of the nomadic Manchu tribes; and K'ang-hsi (r. 1662-1722), the second Manchu Emperor of China, regarded them as under Manchu suzerainty. During the mid 1640s, the first years of Manchu rule in China, the Manchu Government was not secure enough to risk a direct confrontation with the advancing Russians over the Amur territories. By the mid 1680s, however, the Manchus felt strong enough to take on the Russians. During these first years of K'ang-hsi's campaign against the Russians on the Amur, the Manchu soldiers detstroyed all the Russian settlements and towns on the Amur and its tributaries. The town of Albazin (Yagasa in the Tungus language, so named after the Dagor chief Albaza, who was the first of the Tungus princes to submit to the Tsar in the summer of 1651), which had been built by the Russians on the Amur in 1665, alone remained in Russian hands.

For establishing peace, especially for settling the "bounds" of the two empires, China and Russia concluded a 6-Article treaty at Nerchinsk near the mouth of the Nercha River on 27 August 1689.[1]

---

[1]Joseph Sebes, *The Jesuits and the Sino-Russian Treaty of Nerehinsk (1689)* (Rome, 1961), pp. 281-7.

This treaty, the first ever to be signed by China with a Western Power, adopted the Argun River, the great tributary of the Amur, as the Sino-Russian boundary in the Upper Amur region on the geographical principle of watershed. Article I of the Nerchinsk Treaty states that "... the boudary from the source of that river [Gorbitza] to the sea will run along the top of the [Khingan] range of mountains in which the river rises. The limits of the two empires will be divided in such a way that the valleys of all the rivers and streams flowing from the southern slopes of these mountains to join the Amur shall belong to the empire of China, while the valleys of all the rivers flowing from the northern slopes of these mountains will similarly belong to the empire of Muscovy...."

Further, the treaty allowed the Russians the right of free travel and trade under passport in China. The Russians in turn agreed to abandon Albazin, and also to withdraw behind the Argun and beyond the watershed.

China and Russia concluded an 11-Article treaty on boundaries and trade at Kiakhta on the Mongolian-Russian border on 21 October 1727 mainly to settle the boundary from the headwaters of the Yenisei River westwards through the trade mart of Kiakhta to Kokand. This treaty settled the central (Mongolian) section—which itself was more than a thousand miles long—of China's boundary with Russia. This Treaty of 1727, with the supplementary convention of 18 October 1768, regulated the traffic across the Kiakhta border and was especially of help in checking brigandage and other similar hazards on the Mongolian section of the Sino-Russian boundary. Also, by according formal recognition to the Russian ecclesiastic and diplomatic mission in Peking (in existence since 1716), it brought in handsome dividends eventually for Russian diplomacy and trade. The boundary that it established remained stable until the 1920s.

Under the active rule of Nikolai Nikolayevich Muravyev-Amurskii, Governor-General of Siberia from 1847 onwards and the driving force behind Russian policy towards China in the mid-nineteenth century, the Russians explored the Amur without reference to China, and established settlements on its banks. Nikolayevsk and Marrinsk were founded in 1851, and Aleksandrovsk and Konstantinovsk were established on the sea-coast in 1853—all in the territory which, according to the Treaty of 1689, was Chinese. The 3-Article treaty of friendship and boundaries between China and Russia signed at Aigun on the Manchurian side of the Amur on 29 May 1858, which regularized these new conditions, adopted the Amur as the boundary between China and Russia.   Article 3, which related to the frontier, said that all that lay along and beyond the northern (left) bank of the Amur and Sungari rivers from the Argun fork to the sea was Russian and that all the land on the southern (right) bank as far down as the Ussuri River was Chinese, but left undecided the question of sovereignty over the great river and its islands.   This treaty also excluded other countries from the right of navigation on the Amur, the Sungari, and the Ussuri rivers.

The 15-Article Sino-Russian Additional Treaty signed in Peking on 2 November 1860, which incorporated the terms of the Treaty of Aigun, defined in general terms the entire Sino-Russian boundary from the Changpai mountains in the east to the Pamir mountains in the west.   However, it fixed in specific terms limits of the two countries in the territory from the Ussuri to a portion of the Changapi watershed as far as the Tumen River which had been held in common since the boundary settlement of 1858, and allocated it to Russia. This settlement also included the 11-mile-long Korean section of China's boundary with Russia from the China-Korea-Russia trijunction along the lower Tumen to the Sea of Japan and allocated the trans-Tumen wilderness to Russia.   Kabharovsk, which lies below the Amur-Ussuri confluence, and Vladivostok ("Ruler of the East") which lies near the Korean border and which is Russia's first large ice-free port on the Pacific seaboard, also opened in the year 1860. In the western sector, the Treaty of 1860 fixed the boundary line more exactly than the Treaty of 1727 had done.   It also signified China's acquiescence in the Russian annexation of the Central Asian Kingdoms.   The British interest in these Central Asian kingdoms was as yet not powerful enough to make them react in any significant manner to Russia's expansion there.

Neither of the two treaties mentioned above has anything to say on the islands.   However, in the interest of clarity, the frontier is marked in red on the maps attached to the treaties.   Indeed, the map attached to the Treaty of 1860 was signed and delivered by China to Russia on the occasion of the signing of the treaty on the Ussuri boundary on 16 June 1861 (*vide* Article 3 of the Treaty of Peking).

The protocol drawn up in accordance with the terms of the treaty of 1860 and signed in Chuguchak on 25 September 1864 defined in detail the Sino-Russian boundary in the western sector.   This protocol opened Kashgar to Russian trade, and provided for reciprocal consular representation for the two countries for the first time.

To put a stop to anarchy in eastern Turkistan in the wake of the rise of Buzurg Khan in 1865 and also to forestall Atalik Ghazi Yakub Beg's designs on regions north of Kashgar, Yarkand, and Khotan, Russian troops under orders from General Konstantin Petrovich von Kuafmann, Governor-General of western Turkistan from 1867 to 1881, occupied the fertile Upper Ili Valley in 1871 and held it for ten years (i.e. up to 1881). A 18-Article treaty, signed in Livadia on the Black Sea on 2 October 1879, restored to China the greater part of the Ili territory on payment to Russia of five million roubles as indemnity for occupation. Further, it left the Tekes Valley in the possession of Russia. When the terms of the Treaty, of Livadia became known in China, it provoked widespread opposition to the territorial concessions. Li Hung-chang, Tso Tsung-t' ang, Chang Chih-tung, and other leading militarists and statesmen were among those who led the opposition. Prince Ch'un, Emperor Kuang-hsu's father, joined the group demanding full restitution by Russia. And for some months the danger of war steadily increased. The Government of China renounced the Treaty of Livadia by a decree on 19 February 1880. It impeached Ch'ang-hou, who had negotiated it, and the Board of Punishments sentenced him to death on 3 March 1880 for treason. However, on calmer counsels prevailing, Ch' ang-hou was reprieved and eventually released.

On 12 February 1881, China and Russia concluded a treaty in St Petersburg and settled the dispute by providing for the return to China the entire Ili country including the Tekes Valley. China agreed to pay to Russia by way of indemnity for occupation nine million metallic roubles instead of the five million previously agreed. The treaty also provided for additional consultates for Russia and China. The Sino-Russian boundary thus established has remained unchanged ever since.

After the Russian setback in the Russo-Japanese War of 1904-5, China started treating Russia with disregard. In consequence there arose several disputes with regard to the long Sino-Russian frontier. Russia made a series of demands to secure the full enjoyment of what the Treaty of 1881 had awarded to it. Finally it delivered an ultimatum to China on 24 March 1911. China gave in and accepted the Russian demands completely. The treaty fixing the central northern section of the Sino-Russian land and river boundary, signed in Tsitsihar on 20 December 1911, delimited the Mongolian section of the boundary from Tarbaga Dagh to Abahaitu, and further along the Mutnoi tributary up to the Argun, and thence along the Argun to the Amur.

The Chinese role in the subversive efforts made by certain imperialist Powers to overthrow the world's first Communist Government in Russia during its first few years in power, the support it extended to the White Guard organizations by advancing moneys from out of the Boxer Indemnity it owed, and its use of Mongolian territory for attacks on Soviet Russia prevented the normalization of relations between China and Soviet Russia for some time. However, the Soviet Government succeeded in mid 1922 in establishing diplomatic relations with China on the basis of its well-known declaration of 25 July 1919, i.e. by renouncing all treaties and exactions which the Tsarist Government had imposed on China. This eventually led to the conclusion of a 15-Article agreement between the Soviet Union and China in Peking on 31 May 1924. This agreement, concluded on the basis of equality, settled questions, including (*vide* Article 5) the regulation of the Sino-Soviet boundary.

Till Japan established its ascendancy in north-east China and the State of Manchukuo was set up in 1932, Sino-Soviet frontier relations continued to remain normal and peaceful. With the arrival of the Japanese army, many clashes occurred on the Soviet-Manchurian frontier. To prevent incidents on the Soviet-Manchurian frontier, which could not but exert a most direct influence on the relations between Japan and the Soviet Union, the Soviet Government presented, on 15 August 1935, a draft convention for establishing joint Soviet-Manchuria frontier committee. On 16 March 1936, the Japanese Government proposed the formation of a joint commission to redemarcate part of the Soviet-Manchurian frontier from Lake Khanka near the Upper Ussuri Valley to the river Tumen, where China meets Korea, and to settle frontier disputes. The Soviet Government endorsed the Japanese proposal and also suggested the formation of a commission with like functions for the Manchurian-Mongolian frontier in view of the gravity of the situation created by Japanese-Manchurian attacks across the Manchurian-Mongolian frontier on Mongolian territory. The Soviet Government spoke for the Mongolian Government by virtue of its undertaking to help the Mongolian People's Republic (MPR) in the event of any attack by a third party (*vide* the pact of mutual assistance signed in Ulan

Bator on 12 March 1936).[2]   The Japanese raised certain objections which held up negotiations and delayed the formation of the commission.   These objections related to the two basic conditions advanced by the Soviet Government, namely that the two parties should, prior to the formation of the commission, agree to respect the Soviet-Manchurian frontier as established by the Sino-Soviet Agreement of 1924 and take measures to prevent any violation of it and that the commission should be composed of Soviet representatives on the one side and Japanese or Manchurian or Japanese-Manchurian representatives on the other.   Japan insisted that it should be represented on the commission as a third party.   This was not acceptable to the Soviet Government.   Eventually, however, the two sides reached agreement, and the joint commission was formed.

The situation in regard to certain islands in the Amur, approximately 150 kilometres below Blagoveshchenk, the administrative centre of Amur Oblast, created tension between Japan and the Soviet Union during the first half of 1937.   The Japanese Government sent its armed forces to the Bolshoi island in the Amur.   It held that, since the Amur formed the boundary between Manchukuo and the Soviet Union and the frontier lay along the river channel, the islands, which were south of the channel, should belong to Manchukuo.   In the opinion of the Soviet Government, on the contrary, the river channel at the time of the Aigun and Peking treaties of 1858 and 1860 respectively ran south of the islands.   Even if it had changed its course since 1860, that did not imply or warrant an automatic transfer of the islands to Manchukuo: it was a question to be settled by negotiation and not by military means.   Fortunately, however, the two parties consented to withdraw their armed forces from the islands in question, and this averted the conflict for a time.   Soon there occurred fresh frontier incidents especially in the Korean-Manchurian-Soviet frontier area in mid 1938, and the Soviet attitude stiffened.   The Japanese, therefore, decided to stop their incursions into Soviet territory.

Despite this settlement of the Sino-Russian boundary by treaties, there still exist several border disputes between China and the USSR. For instance, besides the dispute over the Ussuri islands, there is a dispute over the Amur islands as well, and Chinese maps consistently

[2]Jane Degras, ed., *Soviet Documents on Foreign Policy 1933-1941* (London, 1953), vol. 3, pp 147-8.

show them as part of China. The *Sheng Pao* atlas of 1933 shows as part of China several hundred miles of the Pamir frontier territory of the USSR to the west of the present location of the Sino-Soviet boundary in those parts. Indeed, as recently as 1953, Chinese maps, particularly the map in *A Brief History of Modern China* by Liu Pei-hua (Peking, 1953; reprinted, 1954) showed large chunks of Soviet territory along the entire Amur and Pamir regions as part of China. The disputes have so far defied solution, and, indeed, they have become more complicated than ever before on account of other, larger issues in the relations between the two states.

MPR Sector

The Sino-MPR boundary, which marches for over 2,000 miles from the China-MPR-USSR trijunction in the east to the China-MPR-USSR trijunction in the west, traces mostly through the inaccessible Gobi. The Sino-MPR boundary on the north-east lies between the pastures of the Mongol tribes and the agricultural lands of Chinese immigrants from the Hopei (Chihli before 1928) and Shantung provinces. This section of the boundary runs north-west and south-west across the Khingan range and turns sharply eastward at 47°N to the Nonni River, which rises on the eastern slopes of the Khingan mountains north of Tsitsihar. Thence it trends in a south-westerly direction to the valley of the Sharamuren, the head waters of the Liao River. Diverse environmental circumstances condition life and activity on this section of the Sino-MPR border. The highly inaccessible Khingan mountains, which run from the north to the south (i.e. from 117° E to 121° E) across Heilungkiang, the Inner Mongolian Autonomous Region and the MPR, are an integral part of the mountain system with northeast-southwest structures up to Lake Baikal in the Soviet Union. The Barga steppe, the grassland projection of the great Gobi inhabited largely by nomadic tribes and placed under Chinese control on 24 October 1915, is ethnically a part of the sovereign Mongol land.

Article 11 of the 22-Article Sino-Mongolian-Russian agreement, signed at Kiakhta on 7 June 1915, confirmed the terms of the Sino-Russian agreement on an autonomous Mongolia and provided for a formal delimitation of the boundary between China and Mongolia by a joint Sino-Mongolian-Russian commission within two years from the date of the signature of that agreement.

The ascendancy of Japan in north-east China in the early 1930s and its interest in the MPR led to many border incidents.   Disputes over fishing and watering rights in the Mongolian-Manchurian boundary along lake Buir Nor-lake Dalai Nor section eventually led to frontier clashes   over the alignment of the boundary between Mongolia and Manchukuo.   On 15 September 1939, consequent on Japan's decisive defeat in the battles waged by it against the MPR during the previous four months, Japan and the USSR signed an agreement in Moscow ending the conflict on the Mongolian-Manchurian frontier and agreeing on the setting up of a joint commission to demarcate a precise frontier between the MPR and Manchukuo in the area of the conflict.   On 19 November 1939, the USSR, the MPR, and Japan signed an agreement on the composition, functions, and area of operation of the commission consisting of two representatives of the USSR and the MPR on the one hand and two representatives of Japan and Manchukuo on the other.   The commission, which met in Chita in the USSR and in Harbin in Manchukuo respectively, reached an agreement in May 1942.   The MPR received the fullest measure of Soviet aid, including military aid, in defending its borders against Japanese aggression in 1939 as well as in negotiating the 1942 boundary agreement with Japan in accordance with the terms of the 4-Article Soviet-Mongolian mutual assistance protocol signed in Ulan Bator on 12 March 1936, which had been conditioned by the Soviet experience of the Japanese occupation of Siberia as far west as Lake Baikal from 1918 to 1922.

The imprecise nature of the alignment in the western section of the Sino-MPR boundary also led to clashes between China, the MPR, and the USSR.   On 5 June 1947, China accused the MPR of intruding deep into the frontier area of Peitashan, 20 miles within Sinkiang from the border according to the Chinese but 15 miles within the MPR from the border according to the Mongols.

On 26 December 1962, China and the MPR signed in Peking a boundary agreement concerning the definition and delineation of their common boundary.   The terms of this agreement have not yet been made known.   Nor have China and the MPR published cartographical details of their boundary agreement.   Maps previously published in China on the one hand and in the MPR and the USSR on the other have shown wide discrepancies in respect of almost the entire China-MPR border.   Joint boundary teams, however, surveyed and delineated on the ground the alignment agreed upon in maps.

The Sino-MPR boundary is political for the greater part, with no reference to ethnical or geographical features.

KOREA SECTOR

The Sino-Korean boundary from the China-Korea junction to the China-Korea-USSR trijunction separates the Chinese frontier provinces of Shenyang (known as Fengtien before 1928 and as Liaoning ever since) and Kirin from the northern frontier parts of Korea.

The Yalu and the Tumen (known as Tomanko in Korean) rivers, the sources of which almost meet in the highest summits of the 8,000-foot high Changpaishan ("Ever White Mountains"), the culminating point of the border between Korea and the region of the Amur River (known as Heilungkiang, "Black Dragon River," in Chinese) form the neat river boundary between China and Korea. The range running southwards from the Changpaishan range divides Korea into two distinct parts: the narrow eastern strip, fertile though inaccessible, between it and the Sea of Japan and the eastern broad strip, rich though hilly, between it and the Yellow Sea.

Korea has been strategically important for China, Japan, and Russia in modern times. Up to the middle of the nineteenth century, Japan was too weak to challenge China's position in Korea, and Russia's interest in East Asia was minimal. China's determination to maintain suzerainty over Korea at any cost always frustrated Japanese efforts to establish diplomatic relations with it. After 1870, Japan succeeded in making a breakthrough in East Asia, and its interest in Korea also grew. It found China's attitude to be conciliatory so long as it showed itself willing to respect China's suzerainty over Korea. In 1876, therefore, it recognized Korea as a sovereign state with full power to conduct its own affairs under China's overlordship. Before the end of the nineteenth century, Japan replaced China as Korea's overlord.

The Treaty of Peace signed by Japan and Russia in Portsmouth (New Hampshire, USA) on 5 September 1905 under the good offices of President Theodore Roosevelt, which concluded the Russo-Japanese War of 1904-5, established Japan's supremacy over Korea and recognized Japanese ascendancy in north-east China across the Yalu River. A secret convention accompanying the Russo-Japanese convention of 30 July 1907 delimited the Japanese and Russian spheres of influence in north-east China. The line of this boundary ran "from the meridian of Vladivostok west to the Sungari river, thence northwards along that river to its junction with the Nonni, which latter stream it followed to the mouth of the Tolo; westward up the course of the Tolo to its source, and from there straight west into Inner Mongolia to the longitude of Peking."[3]   North of this line Russia was to have a free hand; south of it, Japan.

On 4 September 1909 China and Japan settled a dispute over a portion of the Korean boundary along Chientao (Kanto in Korean) in the north-east corner of Kirin by concluding an agreement which recognized the Tumen River as the boundary between China and Korea there.   The boundary line in the region of the source of the Tumen started, according to Article 1 of this agreement, from the boundary monument, thence following the course of the Shih-yi River.   Japan gave away this frontier region over to China in exchange for important railway concessions in north-east China.

There is no specific boundary dispute between China and Korea except for the Changpaishan section of the Yalu-Tumen border. Chinese maps show this entire massif as part of China, whereas Korean maps show it to be right on the boundary between the two countries.

VIETNAM SECTOR

The Sino-Vietnamese boundary from the China-Vietnam conterminus along the Gulf of Tongking to the China-Laos-Vietnam trijunction separates the Chinese frontier provinces of Kwangsi and Yunnan and the Vietnamese frontier part of Tongking, north Vietnam.

Following the establishment of the French protectorate over Annam, central Vietnam, by a treaty signed in Qui Mui on 25 August 1883, the Chinese and the French became neighbours in south-east Asia.   Increasing French interests in the commerce and economy of south-east China necessitated the establishment of the paramount influence of France over Tongking which held, so far as France was concerned, the key to China.   The transfer of Annam's allegiance from China to France led to hostilities between the Chinese and the French.   China's dispatch of "volunteer" troops from Kwangsi and Yunnan to Tuyen Quan along the Songkoi ("Red River") in Tongking, mainly to ensure its suzerainty over Annam and to draw the French off from an attack on Formosa, critically affected the

---

[3]Nicholas Roosevelt, *The Testless Pacific* (New York, 1928), p. 130 ff; Ernest Batson Price, *The Russo-Japanese Treaties of 1907-1916 Concerning Manchuria and Mongolia* (Baltimore, 1933), pp. 107-11.

military as well as political situation in Tongking. China's failure to adhere to the terms of the Sino-French convention signed in T'ientsin, traditional seat of the viceroys of Chihli, on 11 May 1884 and its refusal to recognize the French protectorate over Vietnam aggravated tension in the region. However, by Article 1 of the Treaty of Peace, Friendship and Commerce signed in T'ientsin on 9 June 1885, which amplified the convention of 1884 and terminated China's suzerainty over Vietnam, China and France engaged to guarantee the security of the Sino-Vietnamese border.

By Article 3 of this peace treaty China and France also agreed to delimit their common border by placing "landmarks wherever necessary to render the line of demarcation clear." On 26 June 1887, they signed in Peking a convention in respect of the physical demarcation of the border between China and Tongking, especially the portion from the Songkoi to the Mekong. On 20 June 1895, they signed another convention complementary to the convention of 1887. A joint Sino-French boundary commission established the Sino-Vietnamese boundary in the mid 1890s.

LAOS SECTOR

The Sino-Laotian boundary from the China-Laos-Vietnam trijunction to the China-Burma-Laos trijunction separates the Chinese frontier province of Yunnan and the Laotian frontier provinces of Houa Khong and Phong Saly. The frontier region on the side of Laos forms an integral part of the mountain ranges of south and southwest China.

During the period of British ascendancy in Upper Burma as well as the spread of British influence in the Shan states bordering Laos within the French sphere in the mid 1880s, French frontiersmen like M. Auguste Pavie, M. de Largree, M. De Carne, etc., from Annam and Tongking intensively explored and surveyed the entire Sino-Laotian frontier. These explorations and surveys helped in the definition and delineation of the boundary between China and Laos in the mid 1890s, *vide* Article 3 of the Sino-French convention concluded on 20 June 1895, complementary to the convention of 26 June 1887, for the delimitation of the frontier between China and Tongking.

BURMA SECTOR

The Sino-Burmese boundary marches for more than 1,200 miles from the China-Burma-Laos trijunction to the China-India-Burma tri-junction in the vicinity of the 14,200-foot high Diphuk La and separates the Chinese frontier province of Yunnan and the Burmese frontier region of Mytkyina-Bhamo-Lashio. (*La* means "Pass" in Tibetan.)

The Sino-Burmese border was defined for the first time in Article 3 of the convention concluded between Britain and China in Chefoo in the Shantung province of China on 13 September 1876 subsequent to a Chinese attack on a British exploring party on the border between Burma and Yunnan on 22 February 1875. According to the terms of this convention, Britain accepted the nominal "suzerainty of China in Burma." China on its part agreed to let Britain undertake a scientific mission for the geographical exploration of Tibet. (Britain, however, abandoned the idea of exploring Tibet in view of Tibetan susceptibilities.) The first attempts to delimit this border were made after the British annexation of Upper Burma on 1 January 1886. On 24 July 1886 Britain and China signed in Peking a convention giving effect to Article 3 of the Chefoo convention of 1876.[4] The 20-Article Sino-British convention giving effect to Article 3 of the 1886 convention and signed in London on 1 March 1894 defined the Sino-Burmese boundary from the Mekong Valley to the Manangpum Peak in the northern Shan states for the first time.

By Article 5 of the 1894 convention, Britain also abandoned to China the Shan state of Keng Hung (also spelt Kiang Hung) lying astride the Mekong River over which both the Burmese and the Chinese had concurrently exercised suzerain rights, with the provision that China would never cede it or any part of it to any Power without prior agreement with Britain. Since the 1860s Britain had been viewing the French advance in South-East Asia with as much concern as it had been viewing the Russian advance in Central Asia. Surely, to have France rather than China or Siam—both weak Powers despite their concurrent suzerain position in South-East Asia—as a neighbour on its eastern flanks was full of danger for Britain then. The British especially viewed with grave concern Siam's cession of its entire territory east of the Mekong to France, *vide* the Franco-Simaese Treaty of 3 October 1893. Perhaps the British intention in abandoning their concurrent rights in Keng Hung to China was to separate

---

[4]Godfrey E.P. Hertslet, ed., *China Treaties* (London, 1908), edn 3, vol. 1, pp. 88-90.

their own territories from those of France in those parts.

By a convention signed on 20 June 1895 China conferred special advantages on France in the southern Chinese provinces and alienated a part of Keng Hung east of the Mekong in contravention of the express provisions of the Sino-British convention of 1894.   The British naturally objected.   This led to the revision of the original convention of 1894.   British diplomacy, which saw the hand of the French in the alienation of Keng Hung, immediately set itself to render the Sino-French get-together null and void.   The Chinese pretended ignorance of geography as an excuse for their giving away British territory to France.   The 20-Article supplementary agreement signed in Peking on 4 February 1897, which modified the convention of 1894 and defined the Sino-Burmese boundary afresh, specially provided for territorial compensation to Britain for the violation by China of the portion of the original convention relating to Keng Hung. The British Government of Burma agreed annually to pay China Rs 1,000 for the 100-square-mile Namwan Assigned Tract near Bhamo.   The agreement on consular representation for Burma in Yunnan and for China in Burma (*vide* Article 13) also ended the decennial tribute from Burma to China as well as Chinese suzerainty over Burma.[5]

Between December 1897 and May 1900 the first joint Sino-Burmese Boundary Commission, set up under Article 6 of the agreement of 1897, fixed the boundary between Burma and Yunnan as far north as the Manangpum Peak in the north-east corner of the Sadon hill tract at 25° 35′ N (i.e. in the north-east of the district of Myitkhina). The commission, however, deferred the delimitation of the portion passing through the wild mountain territory of the Wa tribes,   leaving it to further settlement. The whole of the border south of the Manangpum Peak, except the 200-mile Namting-Nalawt section, had been duly demarcated in the spring of 1899.   Uncertainty as to the territories inhabited by the different Wa tribes mainly accounted for the difficulty of settling the border there in 1899-1900.

Consequent on their military encounter with the Chinese in the N'mai Hka region in 1897-98, the British notified the Government of China that they held the N'mai Hka-Salween divide as the pro-

---

[5]C.U. Aitchison, ed., *A Collection of Treaties, Engagements and Sanads Relating to India and Her Neighbouring Countries* (Calcutta, 1909), vol. 2, pp. 58-63.

visional boundary. Chinese troops violated this provisional line in February 1900 and August 1902 in the villages Hpare and Lagwi inhabited by the Lashi tribe. In reply to the protests of the British, China agreed to a joint investigation in March 1905. When China refused to accede to the British demand in 1906 that the border should be held to run along the Irrawadi-Salween watershed, the British informed China of their intention to occupy and administer the country without further discussion. Tension mounted and there was a raid from Yunnan into Hpimaw. The Chinese regarded the Hipimaw incident as an act of aggression by the British. They protested when the British sent an expedition there from Burma in December 1910.

There was another border incident in this undefined territory in 1933, and this led to a serious worsening of the border relations between Burma and Yunnan. The main points in dispute were the disposition of the area of the valuable silver mines on the eastern slopes of the Lufang ridge and the location of the K'unming range of mountains. (*Lufang* is Chinese for "smelting house", so called because of the silver mines in the vicinity which were worked to exhaution in the eighteenth century.) There was an exchange of notes on 9 April 1935 between Alexander Cadogan, then British Ambassador to China, and Wang Ching-wei, Foreign Minister and President of the Executive Yuan of China, and in accordance with the understanding arrived at during their negotiations a joint Sino-British boundary commission was set up under the neutral chairmanship of Colonel Frederic Iselin of the League of Nations to settle the line permanently both on the ground and on the map, *vide* Article 3 of the agreement of 1897 relating to the southern section of the boundary between Burma and Yunnan which had been left undemarcated in 1899-1900.

Japan's war with China stopped the work of the Iselin Commission. There was no way thus of knowing whether the commission had recommended allocation of the (disputed) area of the silver mines to Burma or China, or whether it had succeeded in identifying the K'unming range, and whether it succeeded in reaching an agreement on such topographical problems as the watershed, the co-ordinates, and the geographical names not specified in the treaties of the nineteenth century. The silver mines had always been owned jointly by a majority of the Wa tribes before 1937.

Despite the strenuous work put in by the commission, the old disagreements still remained, and the final map showed half a dozen lines representing different views as to the position of the Sino-Burmese boundary. A scientific expedition from Yunnan also joined the commission for purposes of ethnological and geological researches in the principal mineral areas under survey.

The work of the Iselin commission, however, ultimately formed the basis of the exchange of notes between the Governments of Burma and China in Chungking on 18 June 1941. The two Governments signified by this step that they had finally reached an agreement for the solution of their complex boundary question. According to this exchange of notes, the emigre Government of Burma in Simla accepted, as a gesture of goodwill, the right of China to participate in any mining enterprise that British concerns might undertake on the eastern slopes of the Lufang ridge, provided Chinese interests in such an enterprise did not exceed 49 per cent of the capital invested in the enterprise.

On the eve of the independence of Burma on 4 February 1948, the Government of the People's Republic of China claimed the entire country north of Myitkyina, a total area of 77,000 square miles. What is more important, China refused, after 4 February 1948, to accept from the Government of Burma the annual rental of Rs 1,000 for the Namwan Assigned Tract, which it had been receiving from the British since the boundary agreement of 1897. It thus served a a kind of notice regarding the abrogation of this permanent lease and created in the Burmese mind an acute awareness of the existence of a boundary problem between the two countries owing to the incomplete settlement of their common boundary. Its refusal to accept the 1941 line led to several clashes between the troops of the People's Republic of China and the Union of Burma in the Wakha area of the Wa territory (on the Burmese side of the 1941 line) in 1955-56. These border incidents led to intensive negotiations on the boundary question between the Governments of the two countries.

On 9 November 1956, China first proposed to Burma certain principles for settling the border problem between the two countries. On 28 January 1960, after much prolonged discussion and negotiation, the two countries signed in Peking a 4-Article agreement on principles for the settlement of the Sino-Burmese boundary along the traditional border except for the three Kachin village tracts of Hpimaw, Gawlum, and Kangfang.[6] On the completion of on-the-spot investigations

---

[6]Dorothy Woodman, *The Making of Burma* (London, 1962), pp. 562-4.

by joint survey teams of the joint Sino-Burmese Boundary Committee set up in accordance with the terms of this agreement, China and Burma signed the boundary treaty in Peking on 1 October 1960. The 49-Article protocol, an annexure to this treaty, signed by Premier Chou En-lai and Prime Minister U Nu in Peking on 13 October 1961, describes in full detail the alignment of the boundary line and the location of all the boundary markers on maps attached to both the treaty and the protocol.

According to the 1960-61 settlement of the intricate Sino-Burmese boundary question, the 100-square-mile area of the Namwan Tract has now become part of Burmese territory. In return for this, Burma turned over to China the 62-square-mile Penghung-Panglao area situated to the west of the 1941 line. Except for the area of Hpimaw, Gawlum and Kangfang and except where it crosses the Tulung basin the entire Sino-Burmese boundary follows the traditional customary line, that is to say, the watershed between the Taiping, Shweli, Salween, and Tulung rivers on the one hand and the N'mai Hka River on the other. From the Isurazi Pass to the Diphuk Pass westward, both on the main Himalaya watershed, this boundary is the last 120-mile extension of the McMahon Line, the British-defined boundary based on the watershed principle which the representatives of Britain, China, and Tibet had agreed upon during the deliberations of the tripartite conference held at Simla in 1913-14.

Of course, for this treaty boundary with China, Burma seems to have paid dearly in the longer perspective. For this boundary settlement led to the conclusion of the Treaty of Friendship and Mutual Non-aggression, signed in Peking on 28 January 1960, as well as the Sino-Burmese trade agreement, signed in Peking on 7 January 1961, which have greatly increased the dangers of Burma's position. The trade agreement, we may note in passing, gave China what it had sought after throughout history, namely access to the Indian Ocean.

Nepal Sector

The Sino-Nepalese boundary, stretching for more than five hundred miles from the Nepal-Sikkim-Tibet trijunction in the east to the India-Nepal-Tibet trijunction in the west and never explored or defined except on points accessible from the major Himalayan passes in constant use, runs entirely along the watershed ridge of the central Himalaya. According to Chinese and Tibetan sources, the Nepalese-Tibetan boundary had been delineated long ago. The first demarca-

tion took place in 1792, after China and Nepal reached an understanding and terminated the war they had been fighting that year.
The Chinese General, Fu Kang-an, who received the title of "Great
General for the Pacification of the West" by way of Imperial recognition of his services in the victory over the Nepalese, remained
for a time in Tibet to strengthen Chinese control there. "Among
other things, he had the southern frontier of Tibet, where it bordered
on Bhutan, Sikkim and Nepal, carefully marked off by monuments
made of piled stones...."[7] The inscription in Chinese characters
erected at Rasua on the thirteenth day of the seventh month of the
fifty-seventh year of the reign of Emperor Ch'ien-lung, which corres-
ponds to 26 November 1792, refers to the boundary between Nepal
and Tibet.

The decree of the Emperor of China in 1793, which made Tibet an
integral part of China and charged the Amban in Lhasa with exclusive
responsibility for the conduct of Tibet's relations with Nepal, as with
Sikkim and Bhutan, also provided for the demarcation of the Nepalese-Tibetan boundary: "Let piles of stone be placed at intervals
along the frontiers, and let no one be allowed to cross.   The Residents
will inspect these marks in future at regular intervals."   China also
established border posts and grain depots along all the major passes
in the Himalaya.   It stationed a greater proportion of armed men
and kept larger stores of grain in the posts bordering Nepal than in
those bordering Bhutan or Ladakh.   It dealt with Nepal more strictly
than with Bhutan or Ladakh possibly because of Nepal's defiance
of it in not restoring Jumla to the ruler as ordered by the Chinese
Emperor.   The Chinese Emperor had accepted a complaint from the
ruler of Jumla against the Nepalese annexation of his principality.
Nepal thus had its first bitter taste of Chinese border diplomacy.

The representatives of Nepal and Tibet also made an agreement in
Rasua on the tenth day of the sixth month of the Fire-Serpent year
(i.e. 1857) regarding their common boundary.

In the past there had been frequent border disputes between Nepal
and Tibet.   Many of these were still unsettled.   One may cite, for example, the dispute in respect of the alignment of the Nepalese-Tibetan
boudary in spite of the agreement of 1857, and the dispute over Mus-
tang.   The ownership of the historic, all weather Kuti (Nyalam in
Tibetan) Pass had posed difficulty between China and Nepal since

[7]Schuyler Cammann, *Trade Through the Himalayas : The Early British
Attempts to Open Tibet* (Princeton, N.J., 1951), p. 132.

the Chinese secured control of Tibet in the summer of 1951. Tibet had first ceded this Pass to Nepal as part of a commercial arrangement negotiated by Bhim Malla, a Minister of Lakshmi Narasimha (*r*. 1613-23), with the authorities in Tibet. The Nepalese had also been allowed to open shops in Lhasa since that date, and Nepalese silver coins had been declared acceptable in Tibet. The question of these coins, however, eventually resulted in much strain in the relations between Nepal and Tibet, and the estrangement between the two countries culminated in a war in 1788.

China and Nepal established diplomatic relations with each other on 1 August 1955. This eventually led, among other things, to a discussion of the Sino-Nepalese boundary question. On 21 March 1960, China and Nepal signed in Peking a 5-Article agreement for the settlement of their common boundary with the help of a joint committee composed of an equal number of delegates from each side. Neither China nor Nepal, however, mentioned the fact of the earlier settlement of their common boundary during the discussion of their boundary question.

On the completion of an on-the-spot survey of their boundary by joint survey teams, China and Nepal concluded a boundary treaty in Peking on 5 October 1961 during King Mahendra's visit to China. The protocol, signed in Peking on 20 January 1963, set forth in full detail the alignment of the boundary line and the location from east to west of all the boundary markers on maps attached to the protocol. This protocol, which stipulated joint inspection of the entire boundary between the two countries every five years, says: "The contracting parties shall maintain the boundary markers and adopt the necessary measures to prevent their removal, damage and destruction.   Neither party shall, as far as possible, prevent the boundary rivers from changing their courses.   Neither party shall deliberately change the course of any boundary river."

Article I of the boundary treaty of 1961, embodying details of the alignment of the Sino-Nepalese boundary, described the entire boundary on the basis of the principles of custom, tradition, and familiar geographical features.   Of course, reference to the watershed principle in the settlement of the Sino-Nepalese boundary is not quite specific despite the treaty mentioning Mount Everest, or Sagarmatha as the Nepalese call it, and a few other peaks as points through which the boundary between the two countries passes. (The Chinese had claimed the mountain as a part of their country earlier.)   The central ridge of the Himalaya does not mark the Sino-Nepalese boundary everywhere. There are tongues of Chinese territory south of it and vice versa.

Like Burma, Nepal seems to have paid dearly in the longer perspective for this treaty boundary with China; for the settlement led to the conclusion of the Agreement on Economic Aid, signed in Peking on 21 March 1960, as well as the Treaty of Peace and Friendship, signed in Kathmandu on 28 April 1960, which have greatly increased the dangers of Nepal's position.

AFGHANISTAN SECTOR

The border between China and Afghanistan, the 20-mile narrow strip of the easternmost Pamir country, marches from the Afghanistan-India-China trijunction to the Afghanistan-China-USSR trijunction, i.e. the Hindu Kush-Karakoram-Taghdumbash trijunction at 74° 33′ E and 37° 3′ N.

The Anglo-Russian-Afghan boundary commission, set up in accordance with the Anglo-Russian Agreement of 11 March 1895 regarding the spheres of influence of the two countries in the Pamir region, demarcated the 90-mile-long northern edge of the Pamir region between India and Russia from the lake called Sarikol in the Great Pamir to the Taghdumbash Pamir on the Sarikol range. As a result of the demarcation, Afghanistan lost the provinces of Rushan and Shignan. On the other hand, it gained the *cis*-Amu province of Darwaz. For separating the territory of India and Russia, the joint boundary commission of 1895 assigned to Afghanistan a strip of land known as Wakhan, which lies between the Pamir range in the north and the Hindu Kush in the south. As Afghanistan regarded this strip of land more as a liability than as an asset, the British announced a subsidy of Rs 50,000 for Afghanistan for use in the administration of the unwanted territory. The 10-mile-wide slender arm of Afghanistan reached out to touch China "with the tips of its fingers."[8] This device of the separation of the territories of imperial Powers in Asia, which Britain had first developed in regard to the transfer of the Shan principality of Keng Hung to China in 1894, eventually led to the definition of the British and Russian "spheres of influence" in Central Asia on 31 August 1907.

"Geographically, politically and ethnographically, watershed and

[8]Mohammed Ali, *Afghanistan* (Kabul, 1959), p. 137.

not rivers are the only true and stable boundaries in these regions; and whether in the higher valleys for nomad grazing, or in the lower where cultivation is dependent on irrigation, the possession up to the head waters of each system by one people constitutes the only frontier that has survived the lapse of time."[9]

China did not participate in the Pamir boundary negotiations between Britain and Russia. Nor did it ever recognize the Pamir boundary settlement of 1895.

China and Afghanistan have now concluded an agreement on the position and alignment of the boundary between the two countries. Maps issued by the People's Republic of China claim this part of Afghanistan for China, as also the adjoining areas of the Tajik Republic of the Soviet Union.

The first treaty ever to record the limits between China and Russia was the Treaty of 1689. This treaty adopted the Argun River as the boundary between China and Russia in the eastern sector. The Sino-British convention of 1894 delimiting the boundary between Burma and China and the Sino-French convention of 1895 concerning the boundary between China and Vietnam accepted the same principle of watershed which China and Russia had accepted in the Treaty of 1689.

China signed its first treaty with Russia in the last quarter of the seventeenth century mainly to halt Russia from advancing beyond the Amur and to prevent it from allying with the Jungar Mongols who were then posing a great military danger to China's far-flung western flank. China signed its first treaty with Burma in 1960 mainly to draw Burma within the range of its influence and political hegemony as well as to secure Burmese co-operation in thwarting Western designs on China's southern flank from the side of Burma.

China's boundary settlements and/or agreements with Burma, Nepal, the MPR, and Afghanistan, according to this account, show certain definite patterns. China's endeavour to settle its boundaries with these countries was part of its larger effort to establish its supremacy in the power politics of the region. The boundaries of these countries with China were settled, in the first instance, separately and/or jointly by or under the influence of Britain and Russia. Their resettlement by China now, therefore, implies a challenge to the

---

[9]Major-General M.G. Gerard et al, *Report on the Proceedings of the Pamir Boundary Commission* (Calcutta, 1897), p. 19.

position of the present Governments in India and Russia in this regard; for whereas Burma and Nepal are of special interest to India,
Afghanistan and the MPR are of special interest to the Soviet Union.

China regards Burma and Nepal as too insignificant to pick quarrels
with, but it sees them as vital in the game of power politics.   Hence
Chinese reasonableness in the settlement of all discrepancies in its
boundaries with those countries.   With them China could afford to
be accommodative and even generous without losing face.   Also,
in the context of its rivalry with India, it was in its interest to make
concessions to them in order to cultivate them, bring them within its
sphere of influence, and wean them away from India.   Although
Burma and Nepal were both aware of the real motive of China, all that
they could do was to express their gratitude to China for its overtly
benign posture on account of their own vulnerability. In the absence
of the enormous power that Britain exercised when it controlled
Burma and Nepal, the translation into metal and stone of China's
boundary agreements with Burma and Nepal in 1960 may not be
able to avert a Chinese thrust there in the long run.   China's border
with the MPR is of little strategic or other significance.   Hence
China must have made territorial concessions in view of other political advantages.   Possibly the moves made by the People's Republic
of China, since its establishment in 1949, to wean the MPR away
from the Soviet Union as also the knowledge of Mao Tse-tung's
statement to Edgar Snow in 1936 that "the outer Mongolian Republic will automatically become a part of the Chinese federation, of their
own will" led to the Mongolian willingness for this formal treaty
settlement of their boundary with China.

China's boundary agreement with Afghanistan involves China
with the Soviet Union in a highly intricate way.   The settlement of
the Sino-Afghan boundary may eventually result in a challenge to the
Soviet Union's title to a portion of what is Soviet territory today in the
Pamir mountain country, including even the three great Soviet peaks
Lenin, Communism, and Chaika (Seagull, named after the call sign
of the first woman cosmonaut), even as the 1960 settlement of the
Sino-Burmese boundary resulted in a challenge to India's title to a
portion of its territory in the area of the Diphuk Pass.   Also, the
frontier of Afghanistan marches along the Soviet Union over a
much longer stretch of territory than along China.   And apart from
the Soviet Union's heavy commitments to help in the economic,
military, and political development of Afghanistan, there is a much

longer common tradition, especially in the politics and diplomacy of Central Asia, between Afghanistan and Russia than between Afghanistan and China.

The most significant part of all this is the complete absence of any similar arrangement with Laos and Vietnam in South-East Asia and with Korea in East Asia. France and Japan have been replaced there by regimes under the influence of the People's Republic of China and/or friendly to the People's Republic of China and/or the Soviet Union. Perhaps China will take up the question of those boundaries at a time suitable to it. It may not, however, become necessary to do so. China may just integrate them in the framework of its own political system. In South-East Asia (the mainland as well as the islands between China and India), where China's ultimate aim is to control this vital area through conquest or infiltration or subversion, there do not seem to be many road-blocks in China's way. Instead of the one great Power as France in the past, there are now the three small states of Cambodia, Laos, and Vietnam, which alone may not be able to protect themselves against China's designs. Despite a regular treaty boundary between China and Laos, there are no solid bounds to China's territorial expansion in the direction of Laos. China seems already to be in control of certain northern parts of Laos. North Vietnam, which has thus far rather successfully been able to tread the middle ground between the People's Republic of China and the Soviet Union (thus preventing North Vietnam from becoming a mere appendage of its great northern neighbour), may not for long be able to escape unification with China. Despite Vietnamese awareness of the Soviet refusal to cede to the Chinese any special spheres of influence in Asia, North Vietnam may not be able to avert this process. Besides the history of the triangular rivalry between the Chinese, the Thais, and the Vietnamese in the area—and this rivalry is likely to be confined mainly to the Chinese and the Vietnamese in future—any thoughts of a possible Chinese hegemony would not be unnatural in Hanoi, and however much time these thoughts might take in maturing, immediate developments should be regarded in Hanoi as steps by China in that direction. Chinese maps already show Laos and Vietnam within the border of China.

Korea, which like the MPR and Afghanistan, has common borders with both the People's Republic of China and the USSR, has almost always been under foreign tutelage, whether of China, Japan, or Russia. China's political ascendancy in Korea since 1950 has restored in the

Korean mind the myth of the military superiority of China which had been exploded by the Japanese in 1894-95.

According to the Chinese historical concept of China as the "Central Kingdom", national boundaries of border states as well as of states in contact with China comprehend no relationship other than the suzerain-vassal relationship. The Chinese aid programme in the MPR, North Korea, North Vietnam, Laos, Burma, and Nepal since 1953 is peculiarly reminiscent of the "tributary system" prevalent during the periods of China's imperial greatness. According to China's political heritage, China can accept only loyalty from the states. on whom it confers in return tokens of recognition of its sovereign right over them.

Thus the main concern of China's policy in the settling of its boundaries with most of the neighbouring countries, on terms favourable to them, has been the preservation of its historical image of "centrality" especially in relation to its neighbours, including India, as well as the pattern of power politics conditioned by it. China will not hesitate to brush aside anything (boundary or any other barrier) which comes into conflict with this fundamental principle of the Chinese political tradition. Hence also China's present more-than-mere border confrontation with India to get India to acquiesce in China's power complex in Asia. China still looks upon itself as the centre of the world.

THREE

Frontiers of India

The frontiers of India, which stretch from the great ocean in the south to the towering Himalaya mountains in the north, are both long and wide. Their history and romance are extremely fascinating. This chapter deals particularly with the northern frontiers of India from Afghanistan to Burma and the role and policies of the British in the precipitation and reduction of those frontiers to boundaries during their rule in India. It also deals with the frontiers of Bhutan and Sikkim with China. Nepal's frontier with China has already been dealt with elsewhere.

The Himalaya ("abode of snow"), by which we mean the entire area between the central crest of the Himalaya range and its southern foot, constitutes India's northern frontiers for over 2,000 miles, as well as those of Bhutan, Sikkim, and Nepal. The Himalaya borderlands have always been India's gateways to the neighbouring regions of Central Asia, China, and Russia. The Himalaya has always dominated the Asian policies of China, India, and Russia.

ARUNACHAL PRADESH

Arunachal Pradesh, which constitutes the great northeastern borderland of India from Burma in the east to Bhutan in the west, comprises a vast territory of high mountains and valleys between the plain of the Brahmaputra River and the main watershed of the Eastern Himalaya. Great rivers rising in Tibet, especially the Brahmaputra, pierce the main range here, and high passes cross it in several places. The land route from India to South-West China passes through here. In the heyday of Buddhism, monks from India and Sri Lanka used this great highway in their journeys to China in the cause of religion and culture: Sanskrit inscriptions in Yunnan so eloquently testify to this noble intercourse between India and China in the early times. There always was a flourishing trade between South-East Tibet and Assam over the Rima-Sadiya trail before the Chinese established their control over Tibet in 1951.

Most of the land now known as Arunachal Pradesh was an integral part of the earlier kingdoms of Assam.

Towards the end of the eighteenth century the British first established their connection with Assam by dispatching a military force to restore law and order and deal with the near-anarchical situation created in the frontier region by feuding chieftains. Raja Chandra Kant Singh (r. 1810-18), ruler of Assam, joined hands with the Burmese on the eve of the first Burmese invasion of Assam early in 1817. Purandar Singh, who replaced Chandra Kant Singh as ruler of Assam in 1818, fled to Bengal to seek British aid. The Government of the East India Company helped neither Purandar Singh nor Chandra Kant Singh, although it allowed them to raise armies and purchase arms in its territories. On the situation further deteriorating, the Government of the Company appointed an agent for the entire North-East Frontier of Bengal from Assam to Sikkim on 14 November 1823. In the war between the British and the Burmese, declared on 4 March 1824, the Burmese suffered a crushing defeat. By the peace treaty, concluded at Yandabo on 24 February 1826, the Burmese gave up all claims in Assam, Manipur, Cachar, etc., ceded the provinces of Arakan and Tenasserim to the British, and agreed to pay a crore of rupees as indemnity.

The chiefs of the Matak, Khampti, and Singpho frontier tribes of Assam agreed to give up all connections with the Burmese and pledged allegiance to the British. The British on their part agreed not to exact any revenue or tribute from them and permitted them to administer justice in their respective territories according to their own customs. They also appointed a political agent at Sadiya and invested him with full political authority over these chiefs.[1]

The Ahoms ruled over Assam for six hundred years—i.e. from 1228, when they occupied Assam, to 1828, when they lost it to the British. Their connection with the northern frontier tribes during all this time was rather loose; for they, generally refrained from taking any interest in the tribes inhabiting their borderland with Tibet. After the annexation of Upper Assam in 1838, the British continued for a time the non-interference policy of the Ahoms. The first British agent on the north-east frontier felt that it was very important to bring the entire northern frontier area gradually within the framework of the British administrative pattern in Assam. From 1826 to 1911 there were many hostile confrontations between the British and the northern frontier tribes. The Akas, the Bhotiyas, and the Daflas made many raids on the plains in the 1830s. The British made a number of agreements with the northern frontier tribes, particularly the agreements of 1844, 1861, and 1865. The tribes undertook to desist from raiding the low lands in lieu of a small annual *posa* (subsidy) to their chiefs and permission to trade below the foothills in Darrang and Lakhimpur. A line called the Inner Line was created under the Bengal Eastern Frontier Regulation I of 1873 (consequent on the reorganization of the administration of the Brahmaputra Valley in 1853 and 1872 and the demarcation of the southern limits of the Aka, Bhotiya, and Dafla tribes in 1872-73), and British subjects generally and people of specific classes in particular were prohibited from going beyond the line without a permit issued by the Deputy Commissioner of the district concerned, containing such conditions as he deemed necessary.[2] The regulation of 1873 was entirely an administrative measure, and the Inner Line created under it represented, not the territorial frontier, but the limits of the administered area only. The application of the principle of the Inner Line gradually extended to cover the entire Himalaya from Assam to Jammu and Kashmir.

In recent years, particularly on the eve of the Chinese invasion of India on 22 October 1962, this system of frontier administration by

[1]Alexander Mackenzie, *History of the Relations of the Government with the Hill Tribes of the North-East Frontier of Bengal* (Calcutta, 1884), Appendix B, pp. 395-8.

[2]C.U. Aitchison, ed., *A Collection of Treaties, Engagements and Sanads Relating to India and Her Neighbouring Countries* (Calcutta, 1929), vol. 12, edn 5, pp. 49-50.

Inner Line regulations came in for a lot of criticism in this country. Motives were imputed to the British policy in this regard, and it was alleged that the real intention of the British in evolving the system was to segregate the frontier people from the mainstream of India's national life. This is not true. The idea was to prevent certain people undesirable from the economic, political, and social points of view from going beyond the Inner Line to the areas inhabited by the tribes. There was no restriction whatsoever on the movement of the frontier people.

The appointment of a special officer in 1882 to deal with the tribes beyond Sadiya was the first important step towards bringing Assam's entire north-eastern borderland within the British political system in India and organizing an effective frontier administration. Consequent on Chinese encroachments into Assam's frontier in 1910, Assam's frontier with Tibet was defined in 1911, and this brought all the tribes of that area within the political framework of India for the first time.

The Chinese, who occupied Po and Zayul in South-Eastern Tibet in 1911, adopted an aggressive attitude along the entire Indo-Tibetan frontier and seemed to threaten its security by promoting intrigue among the frontier tribes. At Menilkrai, several miles south of the customary boundary line, they even put up a board inscribed with a notice in Chinese. The inscription was: "Great Pure Empire Boundary, Zayul, Southern Limit." They thus tried to make Zayul the southern limit of the frontier of the Szechwan province of the Chinese Empire.

The Abor, Miri, and Mishmi missions of 1912-13 surveyed and mapped the entire frontier watershed. The principal object of these missions was to establish firmly the frontier between Assam and Tibet. The Assam Himalaya was explored during 1910-13 with a view to gathering the geographical and political data needed to define the boundary between Assam and Tibet. The Government also successfully accomplished the exploration of the entire frontier from the north-western tip of Burma in the east to the north-eastern tip of Bhutan in the west. The Government of India did not want to define Assam's frontier with Tibet until it had obtained full information in the matter. It also came to the conclusion that the best way to safeguard the Assam frontier from Chinese aggression would be to push forward the outer line till there was a good strategical boundary under its control, and to bind the tribes to agreements.

In the first instance, it decided to obtain full information on the geography of the frontier, which was then practically uncharted, and on the nature and extent of the territory of each tribe. It also wanted to find out whether any of them recognized the suzerainty of China or Tibet.

Eventually, in 1913, the representatives of the Governments of China, India, and Tibet met at Simla. In the following year the representatives of India and Tibet were able to agree between themselves as to the precise alignment of the boundary between Assam and Tibet. This boundary—called the McMahon Line after the British representatives, Sir Henry McMahon—ran, by and large, along the central ridge of the Eastern Himalaya. The effect of it was to avoid a direct frontier between China and India in the area. It also gave promise of meeting administrative needs and of providing political safeguards throughout Assam's frontier with Tibet.

During the Second World War China published maps which showed its frontier as almost touching the Brahmaputra River west of Sadiya and as incorporating even those Abor (now called Adi) villages which had long been administered by the Government of Assam. Maps published in India, on the other hand, put its frontier much further north and showed it as running from the Isu Razi Pass on the Irrawady-Salween water parting to the north-eastern tip of Bhutan. This was the situation when China invaded India on 22 October 1962. The stalemate is continuing.

BHUTAN

Bhutan, which lies on the southern slopes of the Eastern Himalaya along the northern frontiers of Assam and Bengal, has always served as a buffer between India and Tibet. The first occasion on which the British came in contact with Bhutan was in 1772 in the time of Warren Hastings (1769-86). Shidar, who became the head of the temporal affairs of Bhutan in 1767, made raids into the territories to the south of Bhutan in 1770. This resulted in tension along the northern frontier of the British possessions in India. Koch Bihar, which was specially harassed and which was in alliance with the British, solicited British aid in 1773. The British immediately intervened by dispatching a military force which not only turned out the Bhutanese from Koch Bihar but followed them into the interior of their own country. By the peace treaty which Warren Hastings concluded with Bhutan on 25 April 1774 the Bhutanese agreed to pay the

British a nominal tribute and undertook never to make any incursion into British or Koch Bihar territories.

The natural northern boundary of Bengal, the edge of the foothills of the Himalaya, thus evolved during the British contact with Bhutan in 1767-73.

After the resolution of the Anglo-Bhutanese conflict, the British made friendly overtures to the Panchhen Lama of Tibet and, through him, to China. The Panchhen Lama had interceded with the British Government on behalf of the Bhutanese during their conflict with Koch Bihar. In pursuance of their commercial policy, the British sent a mission to Tibet with a view to opening trade routes with Tibet *via* Bhutan in the summer of 1774. Though British arms failed as an instrument of economic policy in Tibet—for the success of British arms elsewhere had merely served to alert Bhutan and Tibet, as well as Nepal and Sikkim, to the new Power on the plains of Bengal—British diplomacy made it possible for the first British emissary to cross into Tibet.

But for Bhutan's territorial claims, there was little intercourse between Bhutan and the British till 1826. British relations with Bhutan, however, suffered a setback in 1826, when, by becoming possessors of Assam, the British succeeded to the position of the Ahom rulers in the *Duar* (Gates) territory between the Dhansiri and Tista rivers. By annexing Assam the British put themselves in a prolonged conflict with Bhutan in regard to the possession of the Duars on the northern frontiers of Assam and Bengal. The Bhutanese retained five Duars all the year round, but surrendered two, Buriguma and Killing, to the Government of Assam from July to November every year. This anomalous position led to trouble. In the early 1840s, therefore, the British attached many of the Duars. This led to tension. British relations with Bhutan were further strained when the question of the right of nomination of the ruler of the Bijni Duar arose, but the British accepted the Bhutanese nominee.

The British had agreed to pay a sum of Rs 10,000 to Bhutan and a sum of Rs 5,000 to Tawang every year in return for the Duars on the Assam side in 1841. This arrangement did not work well. There was trouble in respect of the Duars on the Bengal side also. In 1858-60, the Government of India took possession of a territory known as Ambari. In 1863, it sent an envoy to Bhutan to explain its point of view. The Bhutanese said that they would not deal with him unless the Assam Duars were restored to them. Under duress the British envoy signed an agreement on the alignment of the entire frontier between Bhutan and India. He also undertook to restore the Assam Duras to Bhutan and deliver all political offenders and runaway slaves who had taken refuge in India.

Immediately upon the return of this envoy, the Government of India repudiated that arrangement. On 9 June 1864 it annexed Ambari to Bengal as a punishment and stopped payment of compensation to Bhutan for the Assam Duars. It attached the Bengal Duars permanently on 12 November 1864. Immediately after the beginning of hostilities Bhutan supplicated for peace. The Government of India presented harsh conditions. It demanded that Bhutan return the agreement extorted from its envoy, surrender all British subjects as well as those of Koch Bihar and Sikkim detained against their will, agree to mutual extradition of criminals, surrender of British guns, cede the Duars which had passed into its hands, maintain free trade, and accept arbitration by the Government of India in all disputes between Bhutan on the one hand and Koch Bihar and Sikkim on the other. On this basis the British signed a peace treaty at Sinchula on 11 November 1865. In consideration of the Bhutanese cession of the entire Duar strip, 250 miles long and 25 miles wide, the Government of India agreed to pay Bhutan an annual subsidy of Rs 25,000, which was later raised to Rs 100,000.

The Bhutanese and the British demarcated their common boundary along the Bengal frontier in 1867-68 and along the Assam frontier in 1872-73. They demarcated their common boundary along the frontier of what is now called Arunachal Pradesh in 1927-28. By the 10-Article treaty, signed by the Governments of Bhutan and India in Darjeeling on 8 August 1949, India agreed to return to Bhutan, within a year from the signature of the treaty, thirty-two square miles territory in the area known as Dewangiri.

Ugyen Wangchuk, who appeared as chief of Tongsa in 1883, managed Bhutanese affairs in such a way that he became the real ruler of Bhutan by 1889. He showed his inclination towards friendship with the British by accompanying the British military expedition to Tibet in 1903-4 and rendering great help to the head of the British expedition by properly interpreting the motivation and objectives of the British mission to the Tibetans. In 1907, all Bhutanese chiefs and monks acclaimed Ugyen Wangchuk as the hereditary ruler of Bhutan.

By a treaty signed in Punakha on 8 January 1910 in supersession of the treaty of 1865, the British Government in India assumed control of the foreign relations of Bhutan. This was obviously a move on the part of the British to consolidate their position in Bhutan and to forestall any possible threat from China's increasing interest in that country. In 1924, the Secretary of State for India defined the status of Bhutan as an independent State under British suzerainty, but not an Indian State, though its transition to that status could then have easily been effected with the concurrence of both parties. Thus, on the transfer of power, Bhutan was not a part of India; and the frontier of India in this sector ran along the foothills—not, as in Sikkim, along the crest of the Eastern Himalaya.

The Chinese always claimed to control Bhutan through their Amban in Lhasa. They showed little concern for the goings-on between Bhutan and the British in 1772 and 1864, although the Government of China did charge the Amban in Lhasa in 1793 with the exclusive conduct of Tibet's relations with Bhutan, as with Nepal and Sikkim. Bhutan, however, never paid any tribute to China. By 1905 the Chinese revived their interest in Bhutan considerably. During 1905-10, when they had gained a position of ascendancy in Tibet, they tried their best to extend their influence in Bhutan. The Bhutanese, however, resisted their efforts. When the British at the height of their power assumed control of Bhutan's foreign relations under the Treaty of 1910, the Chinese claim to suzerainty over Bhutan became muffled.

Like the British, the present Government of India has also formally guaranteed the territorial integrity of Bhutan. However, according to the treaty of friendship with Bhutan, signed on 8 August 1949 in supersession of the treaty of 1910, India has undertaken only to guide rather than control Bhutan's foreign relations or dictate policy there. By sponsoring Bhutan for the membership of the United Nations in 1970-71 it gave proof of its genuine friendship for, and goodwill towards, Bhutan. It has been implementing a vigorous aid programme for Bhutan's economic and social development.

Bhutan, which occupies a most important part of the glacis of the Eastern Himalaya, needs urgently and speedily to be strengthened. Its northern frontiers with Tibet have never been properly explored and surveyed. The People's Republic of China, which has refused to accept Bhutan as a protectorate of India, has made clear its unwillingness to discuss with India the question of the Bhutanese-Tibetan boundary. The position of the Ha-Chhumbi sector of the boundary between the two countries particularly has not yet been settled to mutual satisfaction. The first efforts to inquire into its correct position were made in 1889-90. There was even a conflict over the customary grazing rights there in 1903-4. The Chinese revived their claims in the mid 1960s. This was perhaps meant to provoke the personnel of the Indian Military Training Team in the Bhutanese military academy in Ha, Western Bhutan.

SIKKIM

Sikkim, geographically the catchment of the Tista River and its affluents down to the plains (including the entire area of the present Darjeeling hills), owes its existence to the British policy of maintaining it both as a window on Tibet and as a check on Nepalese expansion towards Bhutan.

Owing to certain developments among the Tsong tribes in Sikkim in the 1750s and the rise of Desi Shidar in Bhutan and Raja Prithvi-narayan Shah (1722-75) in Nepal in 1767, all Sikkimese territory that lay east of the Tista was occupied by the Bhutanese and all that lay west of it by the Nepalese. This set the course of the modern history of Sikkim. The Bhutanese eventually withdrew. Sikkim signed a peace treaty with Nepal in 1775, but the Nepalese broke it in 1788 and occupied Ilam. The Nepalese were induced to withdraw only after they were allowed to annex the border district of Nyalam of Tibet, then suzerain of Sikkim. The fertile Chhumbi Valley, taken by Tibet during its war with Nepal in 1788-92, also originally belonged to Sikkim.

The Anglo-Nepalese War of 1814-15 brought the British into contact with Sikkim for the first time. Sikkim signed a 10-Article Treaty with the British at Titaliya on 10 February 1817. By this treaty it won back all the territory between the Tista River in the east and the Mechi River in the west which had been wrested from it by Nepal in 1792. The British Government in India assumed the position of "lord paramount" of Sikkim. Its paramountcy over Sikkim was never formally accepted. This becomes clear from the reprimand administered by the Amban in Lhasa to the Chhogyal of Sikkim in 1873, apropos the visit of the Deputy Commissioner of Darjeeling to the frontier of Tibet. (This reprimand is incidentally also illustrative of the Chinese imperial methods in the Himalaya):

Your State of Sikkim borders on Tibet. You know our wishes

and our policy. You are bound to prevent the English from crossing our frontier. Yet it is entirely your fault—thanks to the roads which you have made for them in Sikkim—that they have conceived this project. If you continue to act thus, it will not be good for you. Henceforth you must fulfil your obligations and obey the commands of the Dalai Lama and those of the Emperor of China.

The Chinese thus put on record their utter indifference to the special British position in Sikkim under the Anglo-Sikkimese Treaty of 28 March 1861. In 1888 also there was an attempt, by Tibet this time, to meddle in the affairs of Sikkim.

Later struggles between the Lepchas, who were the original inhabitants of Sikkim, and the rulers of Sikkim, who first came from Kham in Eastern Tibet, caused serious disturbances on the British frontier. The British Government had to intervene in the interests of law and order. During a boundary dispute between Nepal and Sikkim in 1826-28, the British frontier officials who went to Southern Sikkim noticed the tract of Darjeeling hills. The British were so attracted to it that they started looking for an opportunity to annex it. The opportunity came when Lepchas raided the Tarai country in 1834-35. The British intervened, and Sikkim bought peace by ceding the Darjeeling tract unconditionally to them on 1 February 1835. In 1841, the British granted, in exchange for it, an annual subsidy to Sikkim, beginning with Rs 3,000 that year and increasing it to Rs 6,000 in 1846. However, Sikkim found it hard to reconcile itself to the loss of Darjeeling. Tokhang Donyer Namgyal, Prime Minister of Sikkim, displayed his smouldering sense of injury when he imprisoned Archibald Campbell, Superintendent of Darjeeling and political adviser on British relations with Sikkim, and Joseph Hooker, a noted British botanist while they were unauthorizedly exploring Sikkim in 1849. Later, on 24 December 1849, he released them to avoid trouble with the British. Nevertheless, in February 1850, a small military force marched into Sikkim to avenge the insults offered to Campbell and Hooker. The British also stopped their annual subsidy to Sikkim. Further, they annexed the Sikkimese hills and lowlands bounded by the Ramman River on the north, the great Rangit and Tista rivers on the east and Nepal on the west.

Thus Anglo-Sikkimese relations worsened day by day. A British force marched into Sikkim in the cold months of 1860. Thereupon

Chhogyal Tsugphu Namgyal fled to Tibet. He died there in 1863. Sidkyong Namgyal, the heir-apparent, who succeeded his father, accepted the terms dictated by the British and signed a 23-Article treaty at Tumlong, the capital of Sikkim, on 28 March 1861.[3] The treaty made Sikkim a British protectorate. The treaty also established free intercourse between the subjects of Sikkim and British India, and permitted the British to survey the country. The British increased their subsidy to Rs 9,000 in 1868 and to Rs 12,000 in 1875.

The British expelled Namgyal and his blood relations, who thereupon went to the adjoining Chhumbi Valley. The British also transferred the seat of the Sikkimese Government to Gangtok permanently. However, the court intrigues initiated by the deposed Namgyal continued till his death in 1886. Tibet supported his faction and began to interfere in the affairs of Sikkim. The Tibetans even built a fort at Lingtu in 1886. They were probably encouraged and emboldened by the visit of Chhogyal Thutob Namgyal, who had succeeded Chhogyal Sidkyong Namgyal on his death in 1874, to the Chhumbi Valley in 1884. The British stopped their annual subsidy, but even then Chhogyal Thutob Namgyal refused to return to Sikkim. He returned only after making an agreement with the Amban in 1887. This agreement, which was really a petition made by Chhogyal Thutob Namgyal to the Amban, relates to the violation of religion brought about by the entry of the White men into Tibet as traders, and to the protection of religion.[4]

The British turned the Tibetans out of Lingtu by force of arms in September 1888. On 5 June 1889, they established a political agency and appointed a political officer at Gangtok, primarily to act as an observer on the Tibetan frontier and eventually to conduct British relations with Bhutan and Tibet. Through him, they also exercised effective influence in the administration of Sikkim. The first political officer reorganized the whole administrative system in Sikkim; he created a State Council to advise the Chhogyal on all administrative matters and conducted land settlement and forest and mineral surveys. The progress of Sikkim under the new set-up so impressed Ugyen Wangchuk of Bhutan that he too decided to initiate administrative reforms in his country. But orthodoxy and the traditional

[3] J.C. Gawler, *Sikkim : With Hints on Mountain and Jungle Welfare* (London, 1873), pp. 104-5.
[4] H.H. Resley, *The Gazetteer of Sikkim* (Calcutta, 1894), p. xiii.

Bhutanese policy of isolation ruled out all change in that country until recently.

In 1892, Thutob Namgyal again tried to go out of Sikkim *via* Nepal, but the Government of Nepal apprehended him and promptly handed him over to the British Government in India. He was restored to power in November 1895, only after he gave an undertaking of good behaviour to the British Government in India. His elder son remained in Tibet in spite of several warnings from the British Government in India. His younger brother Sidkeong Namgyal, popularly called Chhotal Namgyal, was recognized as the heir-apparent in February 1899, and he succeeded to the throne on the death of Thutob Namgyal in February 1914.

After the expulsion of the Tibetans from Sikkim, the British Government in India tried to settle the Sikkimese-Tibetan boundary with the Amban in Lhasa. Ultimately, on 17 March 1890, the British and the Chinese concluded, in Darjeeling, a convention relating to Sikkim and Tibet which declared the principality of Sikkim to be a protectorate of India. (Earlier the Chhogyal of Sikkim used to live most of the time in the Chhumbi Valley on a stipend from Tibet.) This convention also defined the boundary between Sikkim and Tibet on the basis of the principle of the Himalaya watershed. In March 1895 the British decided to mark the line where British territory ended and Tibetan dominance began, but they failed to do so as the Tibetan authorities refused to recognize the line of delimitation defined by the Convention of 1890. There was no provision for the demarcation of the Sikkimese-Tibetan boundary as set forth in the Convention of 1890.

The Tibetans, who regarded the Convention of 1890 invalid inasmuch as it had not been signed by them, specially claimed and occupied the Giagong plateau, a strip of territory at the head of the Lachhen Valley in the area of the Tista watershed, which belonged to Sikkim according to the Convention of 1890. There had never been any formal borderline between Sikkim and Tibet, and the border people used to pasture their cattle wherever they pleased. In May 1902, the Government of India asserted its treaty rights and expelled all Tibetan personnel and posts at Giagang. A British expeditionary force went to Tibet in 1903, and Lhasa, seat of the Dalai Lama of Tibet, was "unveiled" in 1904.

After the independence of India and the lapse of British paramountcy over Sikkim, free India assumed responsibility for Sikkim's external relations, defence, and communications. India and Sikkim formalized an interim arrangement by a Standstill Agreement intended to cover the period of the negotiations initiated with a view to working out a fresh treaty between the two countries. The fresh treaty signed in Gangtok on 5 December 1950 provided for the continuance of Sikkim as a protectorate of India in view of its geographical and strategic position. India is now responsible for the external affairs, defence, and strategic communications of Sikkim with no interference in its internal affairs, and all this is of course subject to India's responsibility for the maintenance of law and order in the State. We may, however, note in passing that the People's Republic of China, which has refused to accept the special position that India has gained in Sikkim under the Indo-Sikkimese Treaty of 1950, has made clear its unwillingness, as it has done in the case of Bhutan, to discuss with the Government of India the question of the Sikkimese-Tibetan boundary. It has been discussing these matters with the Chhogyal of Sikkim over the head of the Government of India and in utter disregard of India's responsibility to handle all Sikkimese external relations.

The Chhogyal's prerogatives in the internal administration of his State have been not only not touched but allowed to take clear and articulate expression.

NEPAL

Nepal, the major state in the Central Himalaya, never became a part of the British realm in India. However, its relations with the neighbouring countries remained uncertain for many years. Before the defeat by China in 1792, the Nepalese had invaded Sikkim and thereatened Bhutan. They managed to maintain their position unimpaired till as late as the Anglo-Nepalese War of 1814-15. In the space of less than fifty years, they had become masters of all the hills and valleys from the foothills to the crest of the Himalaya and from the Tista River in the east to the Satluj River in the west.

Both British commercial interests and the Nepalese schemes of territorial aggrandisement initiated by Prithvinarayan Shah (r. 1742-75) of Nepal in and beyond the Himalaya were responsible for the first Anglo-Nepalese contact in 1767-69. The British were aware of the commercial potentialities of the countries north of the Gangetic plain even before they had acquired the areas stretching to the foothills of the Himalaya in the post-Plassey years. When, therefore, this trade passing through Nepal was disrupted in consequence of the Gorkha invasion of the Nepal Valley in 1767, the British, unwilling to be deprived of the benefits arising from the commercial intercourse between Bengal and Tibet, at once responded to a call for help from Jaya Prakash Malla, Raja of Kathmandu, and dispatched a small military force to assist him in ousting the Gorkha invaders.

The British force returned without reaching its destination and without achieving its main objective, namely the establishment of a trading post in Nepal. Its failure emboldened Prithvinarayan Shah, who had come out victorious in the Gorkha-Nepalese conflict in 1769, to pursue vigorously a policy of exclusion and resistance as regards British interests in Nepal. The British soon realized the unwisdom of antagonizing him. They were also tempted by the possibilities of trade between Bengal and the countries that lay to its north and decided to forge commercial and diplomatic relations with Nepal. Their persistent efforts bore fruit in 1792. In 1788, following a Nepalese attack on Tibet (sparked off by a bitter dispute between Kathmandu and Lhasa over the circulation of the debased Nepalese coins in Tibet of the fallen Malla regime), the Panchhen Lama approached the British for help against the Nepalese. (The Mala King had violated an agreement between himself and Tibet by not using the stipulated proportion of silver in the coins minted for Tibet.) The Tibetans alleged that seeing that they had no mint of their own and were helpless in the matter, the Nepalese King had chosen to exploit them by putting bad money into circulation; and the Nepalese, on their part, accused the Tibetans of mixing dust with the salt which they exported from Tibet and of levying heavy duties on the flour which they imported into Tibet. The British, who had no wish to be involved in the Himalayan wars, refused to comply with the Panchhen Lama's request on the ground that the distance between Bengal and Tibet was a forbidding factor, that the Nepalese had given no provocation to the British, and that British military help might not be liked by China, Tibet's suzerain.[5]

China did not intervene in the Nepalese-Tibetan conflict at first, but it felt obliged to do so when the Nepalese annexed the frontier districts of South Tibet and plundered the monasteries there. The Chinese asked the Nepalese to withdraw their troops from Tibet and

[5]Alastair Lamb, *Britain and Chinese Central Asia: The Road to Lhasa, 1767 to 1905* (London, 1960), pp. 23-24.

make good all the losses suffered by the monasteries. Nepal refused to comply with the demands. China then sent a large army which marched from Szechwan across Tibet. The Chinese army not only drove the Nepalese out of Tibet but chased them up to Nawakot, close to Kathmandu, and imposed a humiliating peace. One of the terms of the peace was that Nepal should send a mission to pay tribute to China every five years; and in accordance with the undertaking it then gave, Nepal sent such missions to China till the overthrow of Manchu rule in 1911. China always claimed suzerainty over Nepal on the basis of the peace settlement of 1792. The peace settlement also put an end to the dispute over the circulation in Tibet of the coins minted in Nepal. It may, however, be noted here that according to both Chinese and Nepalese primary sources, there was, at the conclusion of the war, no treaty in the form of single written document signed by both parties. The two parties only exchanged letters.

The Nepalese, who concluded a 7-Article treaty of commerce with the British on 1 March 1792, appealed to the British for help against China. In doing so they hoped that an alliance with the British might prove a powerful means of deterring the Chinese from exacting a heavy retribution. The British did not wish to provoke the Chinese for the sake of the Nepalese because that would put their trade with China in jeopardy. On the other hand, they also realized that nothing could be more undesirable than the conquest of Nepal by China, for a Chinese presence so close to British territory might lead to abiding frontier disputes. They, therefore, offered to mediate between the Nepalese and the Chinese and, to this end, sent an envoy to Nepal in September 1792. However, before the British envoy had reached Patna, the Chinese-Nepalese war ended, and the Nepalese were forced to conclude peace with the Chinese on humiliating terms.

Neither the Nepalese nor the Chinese liked the intriguing British role in the Sino-Nepalese conflict. The reluctance shown by the British to come to the rescue of Nepal even after obtaining a commercial treaty only deepened Nepalese distrust of the British. The Nepalese felt that they would be justified in treating the commercial treaty of 1792 as a dead letter and acted accordingly. The Chinese showed their disapproval of British interference in the Himalaya by turning down the proposals of the George Macartney embassy to China in 1793.

There was no improvement in British relations with Nepal until 1800, when Ran Bahadur Shah, who had abdicated the throne of Nepal in favour of his infant son Girvan Juddha Bikram Shah in March 1799, took up residence at Varanasi. The British had played no part in these internal developments in Nepal, but, in Ran Bahadur Shah's presence at Varanasi, they found the much-sought-after opportunity to resume negotiations with Nepal for both the revival of the old commercial connection and the development of political relations. After making sure that Ran Bahadur Shah would not remain hostile to British interests if helped to stage a come-back, the British Government opened negotiations with Kathmandu. No sooner did Ran Bahadur Shah learn that the British were in touch with his opponents in Kathmandu than he wrote to certain chiefs in Nepal, warning them against any friendship with the British. Thanks, however, to the efforts of Gajaraj Mishra, the royal preceptor of Nepal, a 13-Article treaty of friendship between the British Government and the Government of Nepal was signed on 26 October 1801, giving a new lease of life to the then defunct commercial treaty of 1792.

The treaty of 1801 also provided for the establishment of a British Residency in Kathmandu and a Nepalese agent in Calcutta. The first British Resident to be appointed under the treaty was specially instructed to try to forge a close connection between the British and Nepal. He was also cautioned that none of his actions should impair the interests of the Emperor of China in Nepal as it would adversely affect the British trading position in China. However, the Resident himself was restricted in his movements to the central valley of Nepal. Eventually, in March 1803, the Residency was closed, and on 24 January 1804 the treaty of 1801 itself was formally dissolved. Tripura Sundari, Senior Queen, who had been staying at Varanasi with Ran Bahadur Shah, returned to Kathmandu and usurped the Regency, and the Government she headed made it a policy to evade fulfilment of the obligations undertaken as part of the treaty with the British, even though she herself is said to have had great faith in the British friendship.

Bhim Sen Thapa, Prime Minister of Nepal (1806-37), annexed Sikkim, Kumaun, Garhwal, a large number of principalities in the Western Himalaya, and the long strip of the Tarai. Before long he came into conflict with the British Government over certain parts of the Purnea, Saran, Gorakhpur, and Bareilly districts. He wanted to take all British territories north of the Ganga and make that river

the boundary between Nepal and the British territories. Left with
no alternative, the British declared war in mid 1814. They took
Almora, which was the centre of the long-extended frontier dominated by the Nepalese, in April 1815 and also emerged victorious in the
military engagements fought in the hillls of the Western and Eastern
Himalaya. In consequence of their defeat the Nepalese signed a
9-Article peace treaty with the British at Sugauli on 2 December 1815,
renouncing their claim to all the lands that had been in dispute before
the war. They were, however, allowed to retain Butwal and Sheoraj
near Gorakhpur, though these two had also formed part of the territories in dispute. The boundaries thus set by the treaty have proved
durable, and to this day the Nepalese have not been able to change
them to any appreciable degree.

The British gained a good deal by this treaty. They obtained
Kumaun and added to their considerable possessions in India. For
the first time their territories directly touched Sikkim. They also
gained direct access to Tibet, and their ambition to trade with Tibet
and other trans-Himalaya countries at last found fulfilment. Finally
they were able to get the Nepalese to agree to the establishment of diplomatic relations with the British. This clash between the British
and Nepal in 1814-15 brought the Chinese into the picture; for the
Nepalese, who had acknowledged allegiance to China since 1792,
petitioned China for aid and assistance against the British invaders.

The British knew that they were not yet the first Power in Asia, and
they felt the need, for the first time, to occupy the entire hill territory
in the Western Himalaya, to make the central ridge of the Himalaya
the boundary of India, and to determine the alignment of the boundary
precisely and beyond dispute.[6]

During 1816-20 the British succeeded in arranging the alignment
and demarcation of their boundary with Nepal. They hoped that
Nepal, having been subdued, would prove a friendly and quiescent
neighbour, if not a staunch ally. To keep Nepal happy, they
instructed the first Resident appointed by them after the Treaty of
1815 to avoid giving offence to Nepal as far as possible and to give
no room to misunderstanding of any kind. Both to flatter the king
of Nepal and to soothe the injured sense of honour of the Nepalese,
they restored to Bhim Sen Thapa, in return for a pecuniary consi-

[6]James Baillie Frasser, *Journal of a Tour through Part of the Snowy Range
of the Himalaya Mountains and to the Sources of the Rivers Jumna and Ganges*
(London, 1820), Appendix X, pp. 543-4.

deration, the part of the Tarai which lies between the Gandak and Barhni rivers.

But the Nepalese were far from being appeased. They chafed at the restraints imposed upon them by the Treaty of 1815 and in particular regarded the existence of the British Residency in their midst as a symbol of national humiliation. They, therefore, sought to frustrate the British objectives behind the establishment of the Residency in Kathmandu through devious tactics. Not only did Bhim Sen Thapa delay the survey and demarcation of the borders, leave large chunks of land unsurveyed and undemarcated to facilitate future encroachments, and discourage commerce between the two countries, but he consistently boycotted the Residency and shut it out from all sources of information.

Meantime the British further consolidated their hold in India by defeating the Marathas and the Jats and annexing Burma. It became increasingly plain to Bhim Sen Thapa that it would be foolhardy on his part to seek to accomplish his anti-British designs single-handed. He, therefore, sent emissaries to a good many States in India and established contacts with the Burmese also with a view to forging an anti-British alliance. Although the relations of his country with Sikkim after 1816 had become complicated, he subsidized rebel activity there in the 1820s in order to strike at the British position there. He also received, and for the same reason, a mission in 1834 from Tsepal Namgyal, the deposed King of Ladakh, who had fled his country after its conquest by the Sikhs. He was set on disturbing the pro-British alignment of forces in the Western Himalaya and Central Asia; for opposition to the British was not just a matter of firm conviction with him. He regarded it as a practical instrument—a tool—in perpetuating his ascendancy in the politics of Nepal. He used this tool to gain the unswerving loyalty of the army—a decisive factor in Nepalese politics.

B.H. Hodgson, who, as Assistant Resident, had watched for more than ten years the growth of Bhim Sen Thapa's despotic rule and acquainted himself with the position of the Nepalese King and army, asked his Government, when he became full Resident in 1833, to allow him to have free intercourse at least with the King. He also felt that the Government of Nepal should be firmly told to fulfil all its treaty obligations. He, further, held that it would greatly help in curbing Nepalese aggressiveness if large numbers of the unemployed martial castes and tribes of Nepal were recruited for the armed forces of the

British Government. Bhim Sen Thapa was intelligent enough to gauge the likely impact of the proposals and suggestions made by the British Resident and tried to conciliate him by coming to a settlement on the question of the frontier disputes in the Tarai. He sent Matbar Singh Thapa, his nephew, to Calcutta for talks and instructed him to go to London, if necessary. This marked a major change in Bhim Sen Thapa's policy towards the British.

The Pandes, who formed the dissident faction in the Nepalese court, overthrew the Thapas on 24 July 1837. However, contrary to the British Resident's hopes, the Pandes turned out to be even more hostile to the British. The British Government at this time was in difficulties both inside and outside India—distressing political situations in various parts of India, trouble with Afghanistan, and strained relations with Burma and China. Nepal sought to exploit British difficulties to its advantage. The British, clever as ever, used the treaties of Sugauli and Titaliya to annex the Morang belt of Sikkim and thus separated Bhutan and Nepal.

The success of British arms in Afghanistan dashed the hope of the Nepalese to wage a successful war against the British in concert with other Indian States. The engagement of 6 November 1839 forbade intercourse between Nepal and other Indian rulers beyond the Ganga except through, and under the auspices of, the British Government. In August 1840, the British Government threatened the King of Nepal with armed action if reparations for all outrages were not made within a month. Simultaneously it deployed its military along the entire frontier with Nepal with a view to launching a direct attack on Kathmandu from all sides in the event of the ruler not submitting to the warning. Cornered, the ruler accepted all British demands and appointed Fateh Jang Chautaria, a greater favourite of the British than the Pandes, as Prime Minister of Nepal on 1 November 1840.

Jang Bahadur's accession to the office of Prime Minister in 1846 heralded an epoch of uninterrupted and unswerving friendship between the British and Nepal. As soon as he came to power, Jang Bahadur offered them eight batallions of Gorkha troops, with himself at their head, for their assistance in the Anglo-Sikh War of 1848. The British did not accept this offer for want of confidence in his sincerity. Indeed they thought it risky to invite him to India with a contingent of troops. However, during the next ten years, Jang Bahadur gave ample proof of his sincerity. In 1850, in disregard of Hindu customs, he undertook a voyage beyond the seas to Britain and Europe and won the admiration of Queen Victoria. He was the first Prime Minister of Nepal to allow the Resident to come out of the forced seclusion of the Residency and undertake ever year a tour in or near the frontier in the Tarai with a view to making inquiries into frontier crimes and suggesting measures for their suppression. He gave another indication of his sincerity by signing with the British a treaty relating to the surrender of heinous offenders.

Assured of British friendship, Jang Bahadur reverted to the traditional Nepalese aspiration to make territorial gains. The international situation in the 1850s was such that almost all neighbouring Powers like Britain and China were involved in one conflict or another. Expansion southward was clearly ruled out on account of the British might. Eastward Bhutan and Sikkim had treaty relations with the British, and this did not permit any advance there. Expansion was thus possible only towards the north in Tibet. Although Nepal had committed itself by treaty with China in 1792 not to invade Tibet and had accepted Chinese suzerainty over Tibet, Jang Bahadur knew from the history of Chinese position there that the Chinese would come to the rescue of Tibet only when they were free from other engagements elsewhere. By the 1850s Manchu authority in all of China's outlying dependencies was already waning. The Chinese had suffered discomfiture successively at the hands of the British and the Russians, and this had exploded the myth of China's invincibility and had lowered it in the estimation of its dependencies. Jang Bahadur, therefore, considered it most opportune in 1854 to strike at Tibet ostensibly to punish that country and obtain compensation for the continuous outrages allegedly committed on Nepalese traders there. He said that the Tibetans had repeatedly misbehaved and had inflicted insults on the Nepalese traders in their country and the five-year tribute missions to China. The charge may have been true; for Tibet had then begun to disregard the presence of the Amban in Lhasa. However, lest the British feel alarmed, Jang Bahadur told them that his warlike preparations were meant to help the Manchus re-establish their authority in China. When the British learnt of the actual motive of Jang Bahadur, they expressed, though mildly, their disapproval of his proposed action, on the ground that it would create tension in the Himalaya.

After a short period of hostilities and protracted negotiations, the Nepalese and the Tibetans concluded a peace treaty in Kathmandu on 26 March 1856.   The Tibetans bound themselves to pay annually a tribute of Rs 10,000 to Nepal, to encourage trade between the two countries free of duty, and to endure the Nepalese position of extra-territoriality in Tibet.   Nepal did not insist on Tibet's ceding any territory.   Perhaps it felt that such an insistence on its part might embroil it with China, whose suzerainty it (and Tibet) had accepted in the settlement of 1792.   Article 2 of the treaty also stipulated that ". . . the Gorkha Government will in future give all assistance that may be in its power to the Government of Tibet, if the troops of any other Raja invade the country."

The British policy of non-interference in Nepal fully reflected itself for the first time in the episode of 1857, when the British Resident refused to recognize Jang Bahadur, who had then retired in favour of his younger brother Bam Bahadur, in any official capacity. Jang Bahadur retaliated by pressurizing the British in respect of the Tarai in 1859.   The British Government in India and the Government of Nepal reached a settlement and demarcated their common boundary in 1875.   Again, despite Jang Bahadur's numerous services and good offices the British Government in India refused to intervene in 1885 on behalf of his daughter (the Jetha Maharani) and two sons, Padma and Ranabir, against the sons of Dhir Shamsher (Jang Bahadur's youngest brother), who had ousted them from power.   All that it did was to enable them to leave for India with their families and movable property.

The British allowed the Ranas a free hand in the management of the internal affairs of Nepal in exchange for an undertaking from them that they would acccept British guidance in conducting their foreign relations.   By this time, the British had arrived at the conclusion that their interests were best advanced by the continuance of Rana rule in Nepal, and they made it their policy not to do anything that might undermine that regime.

Very cordial relations obtained between the British Government in India and the Government of Nepal in the time of Chandra Shamsher, who became Prime Minister and Maharaja in mid 1901.   The British had not been on good terms with the Government of Tibet since the mid 1880s.   Finding no other solution to the problem posed by what looked like aggressiveness on the part of Tibet, Lord Curzon, as Viceroy and Governor-General of India, decided in 1903 to send a military expedition to Tibet to compel the Government there to concede certain rights to the British in the matter of trade, exploration, etc. Nepal's position was rather delicate in this matter; for by the Treaty of 1856 it was committed to defend Tibet against foreign aggression. Chandra Shamsher, who did not feel it impolitic to ignore the 1856 treaty obligation, at once offered to assist the British expedition in Tibet. However, in the Nepal Darbar (Court), there was a group which strongly opposed Chandra Shamser's offer. When the British came to know of this embarrassment of Chandra, they politely declined his offer.

Nepal supported the British in the First World War. It did so possibly to acquire greater influence with the British and thus to prevent them from giving more support to Tibet. Maharaja Chandra Shamsher also thought that if he were on the side of the British, recognition of Nepal's full independence after the war would become obligatory on the British Government. By supporting the British, he also indirectly strengthened his position and power in the eyes of the Bharadars and Sardars of Nepal because he thought that British support for him was enough to overawe all his opponents. He was not far wrong; for, after the war, he succeeded in getting all he wanted for Nepal and for himself and for his family.

The Governments of India and Nepal concluded a treaty of friendship on 21 December 1923. The Treaty of 1923 declared: "The two governments [of India and Nepal] hereby undertake to inform each other of any serious friction or misunderstanding with any neighbouring State likely to cause any breach in the friendly relations between the two Governments." It specially provided for close consultation and co-operation between the Governments of India and Nepal in the event of any disturbance of peace in either country. The British sanctioned and annual payment of Rs 1,000,000 in perpetuity. Earlier, in June 1923, the British had also withdrawn certain restricting provisions of the earlier treaties, particularly those limiting Nepal's external relations to those with the British only, and recognized, in September 1923, the practice of the Government of Nepal of employing British subjects without prior reference to the Government of India. Despite all this, Nepal's foreign relations continued to be conducted through the Government of India, and the nature of relationship between the British and Nepal did not show any significant change.

A noteworthy aspect of the problem of Nepal which required constant attention from the Government of India was the tendency on the part of Nepal to expand at the expense of Bhutan, Sikkim, and Tibet.

These latter naturally felt insecure in varying degrees. Despite the limits set by the British in 1815 to Nepalese expansion in the east and the west, people from Nepal or of Nepalese origin settled on a large scale in Bhutan and Sikkim. Indeed they now form the bulk of Sikkim's population. Nepal's relations with Tibet were constantly vitiated and placed under a strain by problems relating to the extraterritorial rights gained by Nepal in that country under the Treaty of 1856.

Nepal's constitutional position also long remained undefined. The designation of the British Resident in Nepal, first appointed in 1801, changed to that of envoy in 1919, but Nepal became independent *de jure* only with the establishment of the Nepalese Legation in London in 1933. The British had entered into no formal commitment to defend Nepal against external aggression, but they maintained an unobtrusive tutelage over Nepal.

The developments that took place in Central Asia and especially in China in 1949 had a special bearing on Nepal's defence and integrity. On 31 July 1950, Indian and Nepal concluded a treaty of perpetual friendship and goodwill in New Delhi. The two countries agreed to co-operate with each other, and consult each other in matters of common concern like defence and security. In the belief that India and Nepal shared common interests in the Himalaya and that they were close to each other in their political and social ideals and their systems of government, Jawaharlal Nehru evolved a policy that placed India's northern frontier at the central ridge of the Nepal Himalaya. Owing to the rise of nationalism in Nepal and Nepal's determination to be master of its own destiny, many in Nepal started expressing resentment at their country's special relationship with India, which was implicit in the provision for joint consultation specifically included in the Treaty of 1950, without realizing that "consultation" did not necessarily mean dependency.

Relations between India and Nepal have suffered from the operation of a factor which is not uncommon today—interests which are shared, but which are approached from differing angles. India is nervous lest China should gain too much influence in this key territory on its northern frontier. Nepal is sensitive about its sovereignty. In Nepal, there is no realization, in purely strategic terms, of the disturbing meaning of China's invasion on India or on both India and Nepal. However, with all their outward show of neutrality for China, the Nepalese are under no illusion about the danger to themselves of China's presence south of the Himalaya. India's and Nepal's interests are identical in the matter of defence and security; their peace and security are indivisible. It is in the common interest of the two countries to promote better understanding between themselves, not through conventions and treaties but through co-operation and mutual sympathy in the realization of those principles which are their common heritage.

UTTARAKHAND

Uttarakhand, the northern frontier part of the Indian State of Uttar Pradesh, nestles in the southern slopes of the Central Himalaya. The enterprising Bhotiyas, who inhabit northern Garhwal and Kumaun, have for long centuries been both the wardens of India's marches and the sole agency of the trade between India and Tibet in those parts.

The Bhotiya traders of Kumaun suffered much harassment in the second half of the seventeenth century. There were also the harrowing accounts given by the Indian pilgrims returning from the holy Kailash of the harassment they had suffered at the hands of the Tibetans. All this stirred the wrath of Raja Baj Bahadur (r. 1638-78), who advanced into Tibet via Johar in 1670, defeated the Tibetans, and wrested the control of the passes on the frontier between Kumaun and Tibet. The boundary established by him between Kumaun and Tibet has ever since been the boundary between India and Tibet there.

In the late nineteenth century British relations with Tibet were a little strained, and Tibet's wardens of the marches naturally showed a distinctly truculent attitude towards the British. They constructed a fortified post in the tract of Bara Hoti on the British side of the Garhwal-Tibet frontier near the Niti Pass. A reconnaissance found the fortifications to be constitued of the walls of a camping ground. Tibet claimed Bara Hoti as lying in its side of the Garhwal-Tibet border. The British Government claimed it as lying on its side of the watershed which forms the boundary between Uttar Pradesh (then the United Provinces of Agra and Oudh) and Western Tibet from Nepal in the east to Himachal Pradesh in the west. Bara Hoti is of no importance to any one, apart from its occasional use as a grazing ground by the people of the border.

There was another dispute in the Tehri-Tsaparang sector, which also had never been defined. Tibet laid claim to the area up to the

Gom Gom Gad below the Bhagirathi and the Jadh Ganga several miles south of watershed ridge. (*Gad* means "stream" in the language of Garhwal.) It based its claim on antiquity, and said that the Gom Gom Gad had formed the boundary between Theri and Tsaparang since ancient times. On the other hand, Theri based its claim on the fact that it had actually administered the area since 1784. The area under dispute (elevation over 12,000 feet) contains the villages of Jadhang and Nilang inhabited by the Jadh Bhotiyas of Garhwal.

HIMACHAL PRADESH

Kinnaur, the frontier district of Himachal Pradesh, formerly formed part of the State of Bashahr. The Hindustan-Tibet Road, which passes through Bashahr, served as the main artery of trade between India and Tibet.

Upper Kinnaur remained a part of Ladakh till 1681-83, when, as a result of a war between Ladakh and Tibet, it changed hands. Raja Kehri Singh of Kamru-Bashahr sided with Tibet in this war. Tibet rewarded him for his help by giving him all of Upper Kinnaur, which it had seized from Ladakh in the war. The Treaty of 1681 granted Bashahr the right of free trade and movement in Western Tibet, apart from giving vague expression to friendly relations between Bashahr and Tibet. After that there was a great deal of intercourse between Bashahr and Tibet, especially the wool trade.

Spiti, which comprises the catchment area of the Spiti River and its headstreams, is the northernmost frontier part of Himachal Pradesh. Once it formed part of Ladakh. About 1681, Raja Man Singh of Kulu invaded it, exacted tribute, and established a loose sort of authority over it. However, it still remained under Ladakh. Perhaps it paid tribute to both Ladakh and Kulu. But owing to its inaccessibility and remoteness, it was left very much to itself. The Government of Ladakh sent a Governor to Spiti every year, but he generally went away after harvest time, leaving the administration of the country to be carried on by the local hereditary officials.

The Dogras conquered Ladakh in 1834, and this included Spiti as well as Lahul. After annexing Kulu in 1841, they went on to Spiti but did not annex it. Spiti continued to remain as a part of Ladakh. In 1846, the British transferred the entire area of the Western Himalaya between the Ravi and the Indus, including Ladakh, Lahul, and Spiti, in perpetuity to Raja Gulab Singh of Jammu. Later in the same year, however, they exchanged Spiti and Lahul for some other territories and added them to Kulu with the object of securing the routes to the wool-producing districts of Western Tibet.

Kinnaur and Spiti separated from Ladakh and Tibet consequent on the peace between Ladakh and Tibet in 1684. Nevertheless they went on paying tribute to both primarily to keep open the northern trade routes until the British authority in India prohibited all such payment in the middle of the nineteenth century.

JAMMU AND KASHMIR

Ladakh, a great frontier area, borders Tibet and China. Drained by the Indus River and its great affluents Shayok and Zangskar, Ladakh is one of the world's most elevated regions. The land route from India to Central Asia passes through here.

Formerly Ladakh, along with Guge and Spiti, formed a sort of empire including most of Western Tibet. It developed close relations with India owing to its cultural affinity with it. After 1644 it became a feudatory of the Mughal empire in India, and, as such, it sought help from Ibrahim Khan (Governor of Kashmir, 1876-85) when it found itself at war with Tibet in 1681-83. The trade relations between Ladakh and Tibet were first regularized by the Ladakh-Tibet peace Treaty of 1684. They were revitalized by another 11-Article peace treaty between the Khalsa Darba (Lahore) and Tibet signed on 17 October 1842 (the Dogras of Jammu, who had conquered Ladakh in 1834, taking this time the place and obligations of the kings of Ladakh) and were maintained thereafter through the agency of annual commercial Lochak and Shungsthong missions, mediaeval institutions for the exchange of goodwill and trade between Leh and Lhasa respectively.

The treaty of 25 April 1809, which established an alliance between the Sikhs and the British, shifted the British frontier from the Jumna River to the Satluj River. In his fear that the Sikhs might extend their sway over Ladakh, Tsepal Namgyal of Ladakh offered his allegiance to the British. The British, however, rejected his offer.[7] They also turned down his appeal for aid against Maharaja Ranjit Singh, on the plea that Ladakh was beyond the limits of the British possessions in India. The British, however, gave him political asylum in Bashahr in 1836 after Maharaja Ranjit Singh had conquered his kingdom in

---

[7]William Moorcroft and George Trebeck, *Travels in the Himalayan Provinces of Hindustan and the Panjab, 1819-25* (London, 1837), vol. 1, p. 420.

1834, and allowed him to stay there on condition that he refrained from indulging in acts of hostility beyond the frontier, and remained quiet and peaceable. They also granted to his son a pension of Rs 200 a month in 1839.

Ranjit Singh's death in June 1839, however, put this alliance to a severe test. So long as Zorawar Singh's activity was confined to the limits of India, the British did not interfere in the affairs of the western hill states, especially their relations with Western Tibet. But the moment Zorawar Singh went into Tibet beyond the Ladakh frontier, they protested to the Khalsa Darbar and asked for his withdrawal to Ladakh.

The British and the Sikhs signed a 16-Article treaty of "perpetual peace and friendship" in Lahore on 8 March 1846. The British obtained by this treaty the entire hill country between the rivers Indus and Ravi including Hazara and Kashmir, in return for a war indemnity of Rs 100 million. Further, by Articles 4 and 12 of the treaty, both the British and the Sikh Government guaranteed the independence of Gulab Singh "in such territories and districts in the hills as may be made over to the said Raja Gulab Singh by separate agreement between himself and the British Government with the dependencies thereof which may have been in the Raja's possession since the time of late Maharaja Kharag Singh."

By a 10-Article treaty with Gulab Singh, signed in Amritsar on 16 March 1846, the British recognized Gulab Singh's independence and transfered to him "all the hilly or mountainous country," along with its dependencies, situated to the east of the river Indus and west of the river Ravi. Besides guaranteeing aid for protection from all external danger, the treaty also provided for the ascertainment of the limits of Jammu and Kashmir and forbade any change in it without prior British concurrence.

In order to determine the frontiers of Jammu and Kashmir with Tibet under Articles 4 and 9 of the Treaty of Amritsar, the British Government appointed a boundary commission. It also instructed its boundary commissioners to stop all payments by Spiti to Bashahr, Kulu, Ladakh, and Tibet, but with the reservation that "if there are religious presentations, they need not be interfered with."

While informing the Amban in Lhasa of the change of sovereignty brought about by the treaties of Lahore and Amritsar, Henry Hardinge, Governor-General (1844-48), explained to him his purpose in appointing a boundary commission and asked him to name his representatives for participation in the work of the commission. The British Government prevailed upon Raja Mahendra Singh of Bashahr to forward its communication to the Governor of Gartok in Western Tibet. Raja Mahendra Singh, after some display of reluctance, finally sent it, through his agent Anant Ram, to the Governor of Gartok, who observed that it was against their custom to receive any such communication from strangers. Although he accepted it, he did not forward it to Lhasa. The British Government forwarded a copy to John Davis, British plenipotentiary at Hong Kong, for transmission to China through K'e-ying, Imperial Commissioner in charge of Foreign Affairs at Canton. On 13 June 1847, K'e-ying replied that "the borders of these territories have been sufficiently and distinctly fixed so that it will be best to adhere to this ancient arrangement and it will prove far more convenient to abstain from any additional measures for fixing them."[8] However, the Chinese Government sent instructions to its Amban in Lhasa for arranging the matters satisfactorily by deputing boundary commissioners.

On 10 July 1847, while the correspondence with China was in progress the British Government appointed a new boundary commission. Besides the demarcation and delimitation of the boundary between Ladakh and Tibet in consultation with the boundary commissioners of China and of Jammu and Kashmir, the British Government also instructed its commissioners to investigate the line of trade, etc. The British boundary commissioners left Simla on 10 August 1847 and reached Khyuri on the Bashahr-Spiti-Tibet trijunction on the Parang River on 29 August 1847. They had expected to meet there the boundary commissioners appointed by China. The Chinese commissioners failed to appear, and the British commissioners, therefore, proceeded to spend their time exploring the region.

Thus, these positive British efforts to define the frontiers with Tibet produced no fruitful results. The assertion of ancient boundaries by K'e-ying meant only those boundaries which had been established in the tenth century in a division of the kingdom of Ladakh among the three sons of the king of Ladakh and confirmed in the treaties of 1684 and 1842. However, the British boundary commission could ascertain in an approximate line from Shipki La up to the

---

[8]Margaret W. Fisher, Leo E. Rose, and Robert A. Huttenback, *Himalayan Battleground : Sino-Indian Rivalry in Ladakh* (New York, 1963), p. 62.

Lanak La. It was only in the year 1867 that Henry Cayley, the first British Officer to be appointed at Leh, entered the Aksai Chin frontier area of Ladakh.[9] In 1870, the British Government secured a foothold in Ladakh. The 10-Article commercial treaty that it concluded with Jammu and Kashmir on 2 April 1870 specifically provided for the appointment of a Joint British Commissioner to supervise Kashmir's Central Asian trade and to maintain the caravan highway that passed through Ladakh over the Karakoram Pass to Central Asia. It also provided for a survey of the trade route from Lahul to Yarkand through the Chang Chhenmo Valley of eastern Ladakh. Subsequently, the Joint British Commissioner was also granted judicial powers to decide disputes relating to the Central Asian trade.

The boundary between Ladakh and Tibet has never been delimited. Since 1918 when the Governor of Rudok in Western Tibet carried off a subject of Jammu and Kashmir and his flock of sheep and goats and herd of yaks from the high land known as Dokpo Karpo in the Chang Chhenmo basin, there has been a boundary dispute between Jammu and Kashmir on the one hand and Tibet on the other. The dispute related to the territorial limits of Jammu and Kashmir and Tibet in those parts, as well as to the status of the Tibetans in Ladakh and of the Ladakhis in Tibet.

The Karakoram range of mountains has always marked the northern limit of Ladakh (and India) between the Kuen Lun and the Pamir mountains. Ladakh never aggressed into the lands beyond the Karakoram. On the other hand, there were several invasions from across the Karakoram into Ladakh before the establishment of the suzerainty of Mughal India over Ladakh. After the consolidation of the Dogra power in Ladakh by the mid-nineteenth century the State of Jammu and Kashmir extended its territorial limits to Shahidulla on the Leh-Yarkand caravan trail, more than 32 miles beyond the 18,000-foot-high Karakoram Pass. During the 1950s, the Government of India abandoned Shahidulla in favour of the Karakoram Pass in accordance with its policy of withdrawing its political interest from Sinkiang and Tibet.

This account of the northern frontiers of India during the eighteenth, nineteenth, and early twentieth centuries reveals that while deter-

[9]*Report of the Officials of the Governments of India and the People's Republic of China on the Boundary Question* (New Delhi, 1961), C.R. 3-4.

mining the northern limits of India, the British constantly followed the principle of regarding a glacis, a crest ridge, or a water parting as a natural line separating one area from another. They always tried to reach the uppermost reaches of the great rivers flowing into the Indian Ocean. The influence of the geographical explorations in the Himalaya thus had a special bearing on both the policy and the making of India's frontiers there. Although the British and Tibet failed to reach a general settlement of the boundary between India and Tibet, the friendship between the British and the Government of Tibet enabled a satisfactory settlement of all frontier disputes.

The People's Republic of China started poking into the boundary between India and Tibet after it had gained control of Tibet in 1951. Subsequently it refused to accept the validity of the boundary, adopted an attitude of hostility in the beginning of the 1960s, and mounted an invasion of India on 22 October 1962. Early in 1960, Chinese officials refused to apply the principle of regarding the watershed as constituting the boundary line between the two countries. "Geographical features are related to the formation of the traditional customary line," they asserted, "but they are not the decisive factors." The administrative jurisdiction of a boundary and the activities of its people, they said, are bound to undergo changes in the course of history.

Why this rejection by China of the application of the principle of watershed in the settlement of the Chinese boundary with India? For any settlement of the Sino-Indian boundary on the basis of the watershed principle will not only deprive China of its position to claim areas south of the central ridge of the Himalaya but also impel it to give up several areas such as the Pemako (now part of Tibet, but part of Assam in different periods of its history) and Chhumbi (now part of Tibet but formerly part of Sikkim) valleys, both of which are south of the central ridge of the Himalaya. A settlement of the boundary question with India will also take most of the wind out of China's propaganda and diplomacy aimed at maligning India internationally.

The Himalaya, which flanks India all along its northern confines with China from Afghanistan to Burma, including Nepal, Sikkim, and Bhutan, and which from time immemorial has served as a magnificent frontier wall, is no longer an invulnerable barrier militarily. The strategic position of Bhutan, Sikkim, and Nepal in any scheme of defence and security of the glacis of the Himalaya is especially important. These countries have always served as buffers between India and Central Asia. Under its special treaty relations with the British, Tibet also served as a buffer between India and Central Asia. Though under the vague suzerainty of China, its relations with Bhutan, Sikkim, and Nepal always had a bearing on India's policy towards these states, especially towards their defence and integrity. Until the ejection of the Kuomintang mission from Lhasa on 8 July 1949, China always used to regard Bhutan, Sikkim, and Nepal as irredenta.

The British Government secured the defence of this glacis of the Himalaya entirely by stabilizing Bhutan, Sikkim, and Nepal politically and by acquiring control of their external relations in return for pledges of non-interference in their internal affairs, thus putting solid bounds to Chinese claims and denying occupation there to any other Power. The small military force that it stationed in Tibet for the protection of the Kalimpong-Lhasa trade route under the Treaty of 1904 became, in the absence of a more suitable arrangement with Tibet (and with China after 1951), one of the planks of the defence of the entire glacis of the Himalaya from Afghanistan to Burma.

On the transfer of power on 15 August 1947, sovereign, independent India spontaneously endorsed this policy of accommodation and goodwill towards Bhutan, Sikkim, and Nepal. While it sought friendly relations with China in the wake of the developments that took place in Central Asia in 1949, it revised the old British treaties with Bhutan, Sikkim, and Nepal in order to forestall any psossible misunderstanding between them and China and between them and itself. It also evinced positive interest in ascertaining the limits that China set to its claims in the Himalaya, where large parts of India's threshold lay undemarcated.

All along its frontier with China, India treads a narrow path between the sensitivity of traditionally independent states and its own need for political inviolability. (China and India symbolize two different trends in international politics.) Bhutan, Sikkim, and Nepal have close cultural, economic, and political connection with India of considerable antiquity. India's interest in these countries also emanates from the vital consideration of the defence of its northern frontiers. These states form part of its 2,500-mile-long frontier with China. India considers any attempt on the part of any Power to cross or weaken this natural barrier, whether in Bhutan or in Sikkim or in Nepal, as a danger to its security. It is for this reason that it considers Bhutan, Sikkim, and Nepal to be within its defence perimeter. In order to ensure that these countries flourish economically and progress enthusiastically, it has undertaken to finance all development programmes in Bhutan and Sikkim and to be the largest donor of foreign aid to Nepal. And it expects especially to be consulted by Nepal in the event of any external threat to that country.

Even though it is several centuries since China lost these countries, it still wails over their having been "seized" by Britain and wants them to return to its fold. It aims at obtaining a footing in the Himalaya. It is now overzealously assisting (although sometimes only promising assistance to) Nepal in its development programmes. It also tried to woo Bhutan and Sikkim by offering them "liberation" from India, but the example of "liberated" Tibet was very much before these countries to deter them from accepting the Chinese offer.

Thus, among India's neighbours in the Himalaya, Nepal commands a special position. The two countries are closely akin in geography, history, and tradition. But it is clear from experience that the conduct of relations with Nepal is not always a smooth affair. The strategic location of Nepal between China and India gives it enormous political leverage. Indian diplomacy should never lose sight of this point of vital importance. China has refused to accept India's special position in Bhutan and Sikkim. However, it will not attempt their absorption; for such a step on its part is likely to have adverse repercussions in Nepal. It seems to have decided to watch patiently for the decline of Indian authority there.

The basic attitude of India towards its neighbouring countries, first advocated by Mahatma Gandhi in 1921 (when the Congress adopted its first resolution on free India's foreign policy),[10] is one of goodwill and neighbourliness, of equality and not of superiority. This must now enable the Government of India to reassure the Governments and peoples of Bhutan, Sikkim, and Nepal of its "no designs" policy concerning their independence and integrity.

---

[10]Said Mahatma Gandhi : . . . "Surely, we are bound authoritatively to tell the world what relations we wish to cultivate with it. If we do not fear our neighbours, or if, although feeling strong, we have no designs on them, we must say so . . ."

FOUR

Marches of Russia

China has called in question the validity of its boundary with the Soviet Union and the title of that country to the territories it possesses in Central Asia and Siberia. This has naturally led to sharp differences between them. China has accused the Soviet Union of creating unrest on the entire Sino-Soviet border and of meditating an invasion of China. However, our study of the making and development of the borders of the Soviet Union with China and with countries other than China does not substantiate the charge.

This chapter deals only with the southern boundaries of the Soviet Union, which stretch from the Pacific Ocean in the east to the Black Sea in the west, from Korea in the east to Turkey in the west. They consist of two parts, namely (1) the eastern part from the Pacific Ocean to the Pamir mountains (that is, the boundaries with Korea, China, and Mongolia) and (2) the southern part from the Pamir mountains to the Black Sea (that is, the boundaries with Afghanistan, Iran, and Turkey). The eastern part has already been studied elsewhere. And in view both of Russia's advance into Asia from the west and of the power complex that developed in West Asia in the eighteenth and nineteenth centuries in the context of Europe's Eastern Question, we consider the subject of Russia's southern boundary with Turkey as our starting-point.

TURKEY SECTOR

The Soviet-Turkish boundary marches for 350 miles below Batum on the eastern shore of the southern part of the Black Sea (Euxine of the Greeks) to the USSR-Turkey-Iran trijunction on the northern col of the 16,946-foot-high Mount Ararat, traditionally known as the crown of Armenia. It separates Georgia and Armenia of the Soviet Union from Turkey's frontier provinces of Ardahan and Kars.

The first ever reference to the frontier between Russia and Turkey—the Asian part of it—occurs in the 16-Article treaty of peace signed by the two countries in Bucharest in Wallachia on 28 May 1812 in the shadow of a threatened invasion by Napoleon I of France.[1] This treaty, confirmed by Article 4 of the 8-Article Russo-Turkish convention (explanatory to the Treaty of 1812) signed in Akerman in Bessarabia on 6 October 1826, did bring one of the numerous frontier wars between Russia and Turkey to a close, but it did not settle all the differences, or solve all the difficulties, that obtained between them. Russia had wanted from Turkey much more than a mere rectification of the frontier it had established: it had wanted Turkey to accept its right to protect the frontier it had established, the right to intervene for the protection of the Christian subjects of the Ottoman Sultan in Asia and Europe, and, most important, command and predominance over the Black Sea. In view of its emergence as the dominant military Power in Europe, after the Congress of Vienna (which met from 30 October 1841 to 9 June 1815 at the end of the Napoleonic wars) it had adopted a definite policy of securing the emancipation of the Slavs and the dissolution of the Ottoman Empire.

The first ever definition of the Russo-Turkish frontiers in Asia occurs in Article 4 of the 16-Article treaty of peace signed by Russia and Turkey in Adrianople on 14 September 1829—the treaty by which Turkey ceded to Russia the northern declivities of the Caucasus (*Koh Qaf* of the Persian and Turkish traditions). Till then the Russo-Turkish frontier used to run from Poti along the lower course of the Rion River, then over the Suram Dagh range to a point in the Kura defile, and thence through the Meskhian lakes to the long ravine of

---

[1]Edward Hertslet, *The Map of Europe by Treaty* (London, 1875), vol. 3, pp. 2030-2.

the Arpa Chai, upper affluent of the Aras River (the Araxes of the Greeks). (*Dagh* is Turkish for mountain; *Chai*, for stream.) The objectives of Russia in this campaign were mainly: (1) the expulsion of the Turks from the entire eastern coast of the Black Sea, including the fortresses of Anapa, Poti, and Batum; and (2) the conquest of the *vilayet* of Akhishka Akhaltzik.[2]   (*Vilayaet* is Turkish for province.)

According to the Treaty of 1829, the Russo-Turkish boundary started from Port St Nikolai on the mouth of the Cholok River on the Black Sea, followed the provincial boundary of Imereti, and terminated at the trijunction of the provinces of Georgia, Akhishka, and Kars, all situated south of the stupendous Caucasus. The entire territory south and west of this line towards Trebizon (now Trabzon, from the old name of the site *Trapezus*) on the western slopes of the Plantoken range and Kars on the Kars plateau, together with the greater part of Akhishka, remained under Turkey while the territory north and east of it as well as the entire eastern shore of the Black Sea, from the mouth of the Kuban River as far as, and including, port St Nikolai, remained under Russia. Russia gave up and restored to Turkey the remaining portion of the province of Akhishka and the town and province of Bayazit it had seized in the 1828-29 campaign. Turkey gave up its frontier fortresses, which Russia regarded as essential to the security of its possessions in the southern part of the Caucasus. By acquiring Anapa situated near the mouth of the Kuban River and the trans-Caucasian port of Poti situated on the mouth of the Rion River, Russia gained possession of the entire eastern coast of the Black Sea and a commanding position on its eastern littoral.

The Treaty of 1829 also opened the Straits of the Bosphorus and the Dardanelles to international commerce and trade. On 13 July 1841, Austria, Britain, France, Prussia, Russia, and Turkey signed a convention closing the Straits, in accordance with the ancient practice of the Ottoman Empire, to foreign warships in peace time.

Article 1 of the 3-Article Russo-Turkish treaty respecting Moldavia and Wallachia, drawn up in accordance with the Treaty of 1829 and signed in St Petersburg on 29 January 1834, laid down for the first time the procedure for the tracing of the Russo-Turkish boundary on the map. It also provided for the exchange of Christian and

[2]W.E.D. Allen and Paul Muratoff, *Caucasus Battlefields* (Cambridge, 1953), p. 23.

Muslim populations which might want to establish themselves within the limits of Russia or Turkey.

The Russo-Turkish quarrel over the question of the rights of the Greek and Latin churches in the holy places at Jerusalem and elsewhere in the Ottoman dominions in Asia and Europe in 1852 eventually developed into the Crimean War (1853-56). One of the objects of the Crimean War was to curb and limit the increasing power that Russia had gained in the Black Sea area since 1829. By Article 30 of the 34-Article treaty of peace concluded in the Congress of Paris on 30 March 1856—a conference which formalized Russia's defeat in the Crimean War and settled all questions arising therefrom—Russia and Turkey agreed to retain their respective possessions in Asia, i.e. such possessions as they had legally held before the rupture. Russia agreed to restore to Turkey the town and fortress of Kars as well as other Turkish territories seized by Russia during 1853-56. This settlement also included the Ararat range in Russia. On 5 December 1857, the Anglo-Franco-Russo-Turkish Commission, appointed under Article 30 of the Treaty of 1856, examined the Russo-Turkish frontier in Asia with a view to settling all matters that might develop into disputes between the two countries and described them in detail.

The Southern Slavs rebelled against Turkish rule in the 1870s, and Turkey put them down with a firm hand. The manner in which it suppressed the Bulgarian revolt of 1 May 1876 was especially harsh, and Russia, in protest, declared war on Turkey on 24 April 1877. Russia's intention in declaring war was not only to champion the Slavs but also to regain the territories it had lost in 1856. By Article 19 of the 29-Article preliminary treaty of peace signed by Russia and Turkey in San Stefano on 3 March 1878 respecting war indemnities payable by Turkey, Russia acquired in Asia, in lieu of the indemnities, Batum, Ardahan, Kars, Bayazit, and the territory as far as the 9,369-foot-high snowy range of the Soghanli Dagh (now Pasinler Sira Dagh) west of Kars. Batum was better than Poti as a naval station.

The new Russo-Turkish boundary line decided upon in this preliminary treaty of peace began with the eastern shore of the Black Sea and followed the crest of the mountains separating the affluents of the Hopa River from those of the Chorukh River and the crest of the mountains south of the village of Artvin up to the Chorukh near the villages of Alert and Bechaget. Then it passed by the crest of the mountains separating the affluents of the Tortum River and the Chorukh near Zeli Vihin, coming down to the village of Vihir Kilise near the Tortum. Thence it followed the Sivri Dagh range to the pass of the same name, passing south of the village of Narimar and turning south-east to Zivin, whence it turned south by the Soghanl Dagh range to the village of Gilichman. Then, along the crest of the Charian Dagh, it proceeded to the Murat Su defile. (The Murat Su is the upper eastern stream of the Euphrates of the Greeks. *Su* is Turkish for "stream".) Following the crests of the Alaja Dagh Hori, and Tandurek mountains and passing south of the Bayazit Valley, it proceeded to the Turko-Persian frontier south of Kazl Gol. (*Gol* is Turkish for "lake".)

Russia thus gained a huge chunk of Turkish territory. The treaty pushed up Russo-Turkish frontier further south. Russia and Turkey agreed to fix the definitive limits of the territory thus annexed to Russia by a joint boundary commission. However, the treaty concluded on 13 July 1878 in the Congress of Berlin—a conference convened for the purpose of regulating the Eastern Question within the framework of the European balance of power and in conformity with the stipulations of the Treaty of 1856, mitigated the harshness of the preliminary treaty in respect of the Turkish possessions in both Europe and Asia.

By Article 58 of the Treaty of Berlin, Turkey ceded to Russia Batum Ardahan, and Kars, together with the port of Batum, as well as all the territory that lay between the boundary line of 1856 and the new line described by the Berlin treaty. The Lazi peasants vehemently protested against the cession of Batum to Russia, and eventually they emigrated to the Trabzon area. Article 60 of the Treaty of Berlin restored to Turkey in Asia both Bayazit and the fertile Eleshkirt Valley and rectified the Persian frontier from Bayazit to Monha Mera, ceding the entire frontier territory of Khotur to Persia, mainly to set a term to the constantly recurring difficulties along this part of the boundary between Persia and Turkey and keep open the Erzurum-Bayazit-Eleshkirt line, the ancient caravan route from the Black Sea to Persia. The Governments of Persia and Turkey conditionally accepted the proposed delimitation of their boundary on 22 May and 24 May 1883 respectively. However, the boundary remained undemarcated on the ground up to 1913-14. Russia gave up its claim to Bayazit and Eleshkirt mainly to assuage British fears. Turkey also eventually ceded the forest of Soghanli to Russia.

The boundary line set by the Treaty of Berlin, which coincides with the one defined in the Treaty of San Stefano up to a point north-west of Khorda and south of Artvin, "continues in a straight line as far as the River Tchoroukh, crosses this river, and passes to the east of Aschmichen, going in a straight line to the south so as to rejoin the Russian frontier indicated in the Treaty of San Stefano at a point to the south of Nariman." (It thus gave the town of Oltu to Russia. Oltu lies midway between Erzurum and Ardahan.) The line then turned east, passed by Tebrenek, which remained to Russia, and continued as far as the Penek Chai. Following the Penek as far as Bardiz, it turned south. (It thus gave Bardiz and Yenikoi to Russia.) From a point west of the village of Kara Urgan, it went in the direction of the village of Mejinkirt, continued in a straight line towards the summit of the Kassa Dagh, and followed "the line of the watershed between the affluents of the Araxes on the north and those of the Mourad Sou on the south, as far as the former frontier of Russia."

While the acquisition of strongholds in Asia Minor had much defence value for Russia, it was the acquisition of Batum that gave it a predominant position in the immediate vicinity of the Black Sea. Indeed it had long been a Russian ambition to acquire the fortress and port of Batum, which occupy a strong natural position. The British, Russian, and Turkish commissioners signed a protocol in Constantinople on 17 May 1880 to fix definitely the point of departure for the boundary line to the west of Kara Urgan (59° 56′ 40″ E). They also concluded an agreement in Karakilise (now Karakose) in the Eleshkirt Valley on 11 August 1880 to fix the Russo-Turkish boundary from Kara Urgan to Mount Tandurek on the old boundary in the east.

Arrangements made by the Allies during the First World War promised Russia, among other political and territorial advantages, the Turkish provinces of Trabzon, Erzurum and Van, and Bitlis. In 1917, the Soviet Government renounced all its interests in Turkey, including the old Russian claim to Turkish territory. Articles 1 and 2 of the 16-Article agreement between the Russian Socialist Federated Soviet Republic (RSFSR) and Turkey signed in Moscow on 16 March 1921 and Article 4-6 of the 20-Article treaty between Turkey and Armenia, Azerbaijan, and Georgia signed in Kars on 13 October 1921 specified and regulated the boundary which has separated Turkey and the USSR ever since. The RSFSR surrendered its claim to capitulations in Turkey as well as to the war indemnity due from

Turkey since 1877-78, and agreed to return to Turkey the provinces of Ardahan and Kars, which had been part of Russia from 1878 to 1918, and to allow Turkey free use of the port of Batum. Inhabitants of the ceded territories were given the freedom to stay on or to leave with all their belongings and property. On 31 May 1926, Turkey and the Soviet Union signed a 2-point protocol on the option of citizenship of Soviet and Turkish nationals in their frontier area, pursuant to Article 12 of the Treaty of 1921 and Article 13 of the Treaty of Kars of 1921. Erzurum is now the nerve-centre of Turkey's field army on the frontier with the Soviet Union.

Turkey and the Soviet Union signed a treaty of neutrality and non-aggression on 17 December 1925 specially guaranteeing to the Soviet Union freedom of passage through the Straits. This facilitated the final demarcation of the frontier between the two countries in 1926. Turkey and the Soviet Union also concluded a 12-Article convention, signed in Kars on 8 January 1927, on the regulation of the use of the waters of their frontier rivers by nationals of Turkey and the Soviet Union on equal terms on certain conditions. Pursuant to Article 5 of this convention, Turkey and the Soviet Union signed a 7-Article protocol in Kars on 8 January 1927. By this protocol Turkey granted the Soviet Union the right to build on the Aras River a barrage for the Sardarabad Canal.[3]

For simplifying the on-the-spot investigation and settlement of minor frontier disputes and incidents, Turkey and the Soviet Union concluded an 18-Article convention in Ankara on 6 August 1928, valid for three years in the first instance. For facilitating frontier trade pursuant to Article 7 of the Treaty of 1921, the two countries signed a 16-Article convention in Ankara on 6 August 1928. This gave the residents of the frontier zone of the Georgian SSR and Turkey the right to cross the frontier for purposes of trade.

The Turkish-Soviet friendship established by treaty in 1925 gradually deteriorated in the mid 1930s. It deteriorated further on the Soviet Union demanding in 1939 that Turkey sign a protocol agreeing to close the Dardanelles, an integral part of Turkish territory, to all countries other than those touching the Black Sea and allowing the Soviet Union to participate in the control of these seaways. The Soviet Union based its demand in respect of the Turkish Straits by

---

[3]Jane Degras, ed., *Soviet Documents on Foreign Policy* (London, 1952), vol. 2, pp. 147-52.

showing that these seaways had been used by the Western Powers in the past to attack Russia's southern flank. By 1939, Germany had already started breathing over its shoulders in the Balkans. On 20 March 1945, as soon as the Second World War was over, the Soviet Union repudiated the Treaty of 1925, saying that it needed to be adapted to the changed situation. On 8 August 1946, it demanded that it be associated in the defence of the Straits as the basis for Turkey's proposal for a fresh treaty in the place of the one as has been repudiated. On 22 August 1946, Turkey rejected the proposals. Until recently the Turkish-Soviet relations remained merely formal, but there never were any differences and/or misunderstandings respecting the boundary line fixed in 1926.

IRAN SECTOR

The Soviet-Iranian boundary marches for 1,250 miles from the USSR-Turkey-Iran trijunction to the USSR-Iran-Afghanistan trijunction on the Zulfiqar Pass along the Heri Rud. (*Rud* is Persian for "river".) It separates the republics of Armenia, Azerbaijan, and Turkmenia of the Soviet Union from the northern frontier parts of Iran. The Soviet-Iranian boundary consists of three sections, namely (*a*) the one which stretches from the USSR-Turkey-Iran trijunction to the western shore of the Caspian; (*b*) the one that runs along the southern Caspian shore; and (*c*) the one which extends from the mouth of the Atrek River to the Zulfiqar Pass near the USSR-Iran-Afghanistan trijunction. The Aras and the Astara rivers mark Iran's north-west boundary with the Soviet Union. Section (*c*) separates Khorasan and the Turkmen SSR.

Azerbaijan, the north-west province of Iran, lies in the shadow of Mount Ararat along the Soviet-Turkish border. Between the Caspian Sea and the snowy range of mountains to its south, the great Elburz, of which Demavend (over 18,000 feet in height) forms the highest peak, are the vast fertile plains of Gilan and Mazanderan. The southern Caspian littoral is Iran's most densely populated farming area. The Atrek, which rises west of Quchan and runs north-west and finally falls into the Caspian Sea, forms the Soviet Iranian boundary from the Caspian Sea to the Songu Dagh. The open and undulating Atrek Valley here forms one of Iran's most beautiful and fertile parts. The great Kara Kum ("black sand") desert stretches without a break from Iran in the south to the Amu Darya (the Oxus of the Greeks and the Vakshu of the Sanskrit tradition) along Khiva and the Aral Sea in the north and from the Caspian Sea in the west to the Amu along Afghanistan in the east. (*Darya* is both Persian and Turkic for "river".) From Ashkhabad in the heart of the country, inhabited by the Tekes beyond the 8,000-foot-high Kopet Dagh range, a splendid separating barrier, to Baj Giran (which is on the Iranian side of the international boundary and on the high road to Mashhad, the holy place of Shii pilgrimage), the distance is a mere thirty miles. From Firuza in the west to Kushk in the east, the country is quite open.

Most of the people living in Iran's northern borderlands are of Baluch, Kurd, or Turkic origin. They were settled there two or three centuries ago by rulers of the country such as Shah Abbas (1587-1628) and Nadir Shah (1736-47) to secure the northern flank against the Turkmen tribes, who used to raid Khorasan and harass the Persians with a view to driving them out of their northern borderlands. Shah Abbas transplanted the Kurds, known for their excellence as soldiers from Kizil Arvat to Sarakh. These Kurd wardens of Iran's northern marches organized military settlements along the entire Khorasan borderland to keep guard against the Turkemen tribes. Reza Shah banished them from Khorasan, sent them into exile in southern Iran, and confiscated all their property. After the Second World War they returned north, retook their property, and are now the most influential people in the area bordering the Turkmen SSR. Abbasabad, named after Shah Abbas, was originally a colony of the Georgians (converts to Islam) planted there by Shah Abbas himself. Nadir Shah, himself an Afshar (Turk) tribesman, settled a colony of Afghans there for patrolling the Turkmen border. The fort of Kalat, the greatest natural fortress of Central Asia, is known as Kalat-i-Nadiri owing to its historical association with Nadir Shah.

The Volga River, the great waterway from the heart of Russia to the northern Caspian Sea, facilitated Russia's access to Persia. Tsar Ivan IV (the Terrible, *r.* 1547-84) of Russia conquered Astrakhan, now a principal Soviet port on the estuary of the Volga, in 1554, and this gave Russia access to the commerce of the Caspian for the first time. Tsar Peter I (the Great, *r.* 1689-1725) took advantage of the chaos that followed the death of Shah Abbas in 1628 in Persia and captured all Persian possessions on and around the Caspian Sea in 1723. He divided Persia's north-western territories in Armenia and the trans-Caucasus into two parts and gave one part to Turkey, the other contender for the spoils of the Persian Empire, in order to avoid a war with that country. Nadir Shah, who ruled over all Persia from Kandahar to Tiflis (now Tbilisi) and from the Persian Gulf to the Amu Darya, recovered the provinces lost to Russia and Turkey in 1723.

The first ever reference to the Russo-Persian marches is to be found in the 11-Article treaty of peace signed by the two countries in Gulistan on 12 October 1813. This treaty gave Russia all the Persian territories between the Caspian and the Caucasus, including Georgia, and indicated in general terms the common boundary between the two countries for the first time. The Russo-Persian War of 1826-28 resulted in further loss of territory for Persia in Armenia and Azerbaijan. Persia also lost the rich western shore of the southern Caspian Sea. The two countries signed a 16-Article treaty of peace in the village of Turkmanchai (Georgia) on 22 February 1828. By this treaty the sovereignty of the Caspian Sea passed wholly to Russia, so that the sea became an exclusively Russian inland sea. The treaty not only denied Persia the right to keep vessels of war in the Caspian Sea but also forbade it to trade from its own shores under its own flag. (Persia had three ports along the southern Caspian shore, namely Enzeli, which is now called Pahlavi, Gez, and Mashhad-i-Sar.) This treaty made the Aras River the boundary between Russia and Persia.

Thus, from 1828 onwards, Russia's influence in Persia increased greatly. This made the British uncomfortable. They suspected Russia's hand in the Persian siege of Herat in 1838-39, and feared that Russia's influence might in time extend to Afghanistan also, and pose a threat to their prized possessions in India. Russian dominions in Central Asia in the 1840s did not extend beyond the Aral Sea. By 1864, the year of the Sino-Russian protocol concerning the Sino-Russian boundary in the Turkistan sector, the Russian frontier ran south-east along the line of the Syr Darya (the Jaxartes of the Greeks) up to Chimkent, and then, running due east, it passed below the Issik Kol to the formidable Tien Shan mountains. By another sweeping advance in 1865, Russia captured the entire territory between the Syr and the Amu up to Afghanistan.

Till 1867, when Russia took Samarkand, the inhabitants of the eastern Caspian littoral—namely the Yamut, Goklan, and Tekes Turkmen tribes—had never acknowledged Russian authority. By the agreement signed on 13 December 1869, Persia and Russia agreed upon the Atrek River, from its mouth up to Chat (where it is joined by the Sumbar River, its north-eastern tributary), as the common boundary. By this agreement Russia also restored to Persia all the territory south of the Caspian Sea, including Resht and Astrabad, formerly capital of the Qajar Turks, which the Russians had held for a century. However, the general feeling among the Russian military units which had extensively toured this part of the Russian Empire in the 1870s was that Russia was far too generous in restoring "that precious slice of territory" to Persia and that they should consider themselves extremely moderate in confining themselves only to what lay to north of the great mountain range stretching towards Mashhad.[4] Indeed they wanted the Gurgan River, which is nearly twenty miles south of the Atrek and runs parallel to it, to be Russia's boundary in those parts.

The Tekes tribesmen, inhabiting the Akhal country stretching from the Persian frontier as far north as Khiva, used to raid Russian territories from across the frontier and interrupt maritime trade in the trans-Caspian territory of Russia. They used to indulge in brigandage, seize Persian and Russian subjects, and either hold them till ransomed or retain them as slaves. When the limits of endurance were reached, Russia organized a number of trans-Caspian expeditions against these predatory tribesmen in 1875 and 1879-81, broke up their power, and established military posts along the line of communication between the Caspian Sea and Khiva. It took Ashkhabad at the close of the campaign in the winter of 1880-81. It acquired the greater part of the territory between Ashkhabad and Merv by the Treaty of 9 December 1881.

The pacification of the Turkmen and the absorption of the entire Turkmen territory into Russia led to a definite improvement in the social and political scene in Central Asia. There is evidence that even Persia favoured this advance of Russia in Central Asia in the 1870s, especially because of the immense relief it afforded to the population in the northern marches of Khorasan by suppressing Turkmen lawlessness and terror there.

A joint commission, appointed under the Treaty of 9 December 1881, demarcated the 250-mile Russo-Persian boundary from the mouth of the Atrek to the sources of the Baba Durmaz stream in 1884-86. The line of demarcation proceeded, according to the report

[4]Edmund O'Donovan, *The Merv Oasis: Travels and Adventures among the Tekes of Merv* (London, 1882), vol. 1, p. 114.

of one of the joint commissioners to the Tiflis branch of the Imperial Russian Geographical Society, from the green environs of the Atrek along the Hassan Quli Bay to the rich environs of Sarakhs on the left bank of the Heri Rud. It followed the Atrek River up to Chat, where it is joined by the Sumbar River. Thence it went north-easterly *via* the Songu Dagh and Saghir mountains, touching the Chandir, an affluent of the Sumbar, and following the eastern range down to the Sumbar Valley south of the ruins of Atilana. Passing the sources of the Daine Su in the Kopet Dagh range, it went north-east up to the Arvaz Pass. Southwards from there, it traversed the Suluku Pass and the crest of the Misino hills. About a kilometre eastward from the Kurd village of Rabab to the Persian village of Kherabad and skirting the Doloncha range, it went north-east, touched a gorge of the Firuza River north of the village of the same name, turned south-east there, ran along the right bank of the Firuza up to the summit of the 9,000-foot-high Gulil Peak, and followed the Berdar mountains, through the Gudan defile, to reach the summit of Kukar. Thence, passing by the Aselma range, it descended into a gorge of the Kelte Chinar River. The village of Kelte Chinar continued to belong to Persia, while the Annau defile, with its southern exit, was assigned to Russia. It then passed above the Kizil Dagh range as far as the eastern spur of the Kizil Dagh mountains, descended into the valley of the Baba Durmaz stream north of the Ziraku range, and thence, taking a northerly direction, reached the oasis at the road from Gavars to Luftabad. The fortress of Baba Durmaz lay to the east of the line.

Joint boundary commissions, formed pursuant to Articles 4-6 of the Russo-Persian convention of 27 May 1893, demarcated the remaining section from Luftabad to Zulfiqar in 1894-95.

During the First World War the British, the Russians, and the Turks fought a good many of their battles on the neutral soil of Persia. This naturally provoked much resentment in Persia. In the Peace Conference held in March 1919, Persia claimed part of the Caucasus, including Erevan, Derbent, and Baku, as well as Merv, Khiva, and the territory inhabited by the Tekes. The 26-Article treaty of friendship, which the RSFSR and Persia signed in Moscow on 26 February 1921 and by which Soviet Russia abandoned all "imperialistic encroachments" and financial advantages in Persia, restored the Russo-Persian boundary as settled by the Treaty of 1881. The Russians also renounced their claim to the island of Ashurada in the southern part of the Caspian Sea and returned the frontier town of Firuza to Persia.

Pursuant to Article 3 of this treaty Persia and the Soviet Union concluded a 24-Article agreement, signed in Ashkhabad on 20 February 1926, on the utilization of the frontier rivers and waters from the Heri Rud (the Tejen River, the lower reaches of the Heri Rud) to the Caspian Sea. Articles 1, 4-9, and 15-16 of this agreement determined the precise share of each country in, and established the method of utilizing the waters of, the frontier rivers—namely the Heri, the Chaacha, the Nafta, the Kara Tikan, the Archin, the Kazgan, the Lain, the Chandir, the Sumbar, and the Atrek from east to west. The agreement further said that the waters of the Durungiar and the Kelte Chinar were entirely and exclusively for the use of Persia, and the waters of the Firuza wholly for the Soviet Union.

In order to prevent any kind of incident from occurring along the entire length of their common frontier and also ensure quick settlement of such as might actually occur, the two Governments agreed, on 14 August 1927, to appoint frontier commissioners, five from each country, and specify their areas of operations.

The 3-Article convention and the 5-point protocol which Iran and the Soviet Union concluded on 2 December 1954 to settle outstanding frontier and financial questions re-established the entire Soviet-Iranian boundary from Turkey in the west to Afghanistan in the east. Article 2 defined the course of the new boundary line, especially rectifying the imprecise demarcation west of the Caspian Sea in 1828-29 and east of it in 1884-86 and 1894-96, and thus remove irritants that had frequently strained relations between the two countries. The agreement also transferred the Yedi Evlar region of the Astara River to Iran and the frontier town of Firuza and its surrounding lands to the Soviet Union. The Government of the Turkmen SSR has now developed the town of Firuza into a health resort and sanatorium.

On 6 May 1957, Iran and the Soviet Union agreed in principle to sign a boundary agreement for the settlement of the many border disputes in the Bojnurd area over questions such as border crossing, pasturage, etc. To utilize jointly and for mutual benefit the water and power resources of the frontier rivers Aras and Atrek, they concluded an 11-Article treaty in Tehran on 11 August 1957. Soviet-Iranian relations became deeply strained with Iran signing a bilateral defence agreement with the USA, allowing establishment of US military bases on its territory in the spring of 1959, but there has been no major violation of the 1954 boundary arrangement so far.

AFGHANISTAN SECTOR

The Afghan-Soviet boundary marches for 1,200 miles from the USSR-Iran-Afghanistan trijunction to the Taghdumbash Pamir on the USSR-Afghanistan-India-China conjunction. It separates the Turkmen, Uzbek, and Tajik republics of the USSR from the northern frontier parts of Afghanistan. It consists of three sections: (*a*) the one which stretches from the Zulfiqar Pass on the Heri Rud to Kham-i-ab on the Amu Darya bordering the Turkmen SSR; (*b*) the one which extends from Kham-i-ab on the Amu Darya to Sarikol bordering the Uzbek SSR; and (*c*) the one which runs from Sarikol to the Taghdumbash Pamir. The population in the upper reaches of the Amu, which gathers its waters from the "high mountain-cradle of Pamere" and carries them over 1,500 miles to the Aral Sea in the west, is of Tajik and Kirghiz extraction. China is now questioning the validity of the entire Pamir frontier complex, especially Section (*c*) of the Afghan-Soviet boundary.

Britain regarded Russia's rapid advance from the Caspian Sea towards Afghanistan during the 1860s as a serious menace to the security of its Indian Empire. It, therefore, promptly initiated negotiations with Russia on the Central Asian question, and in 1872-73 the two countries agreed to accept Afghanistan as a neutral zone of territory between their possessions to prevent them from contact and to treat the Amu as the northern limit of Afghanistan from the 13,300-foot-high Lake Victoria in the east to Khoja Salih in the west. They also recognized Badakhshan, along with Wakhan, from Lake Victoria in the east to the junction of the Kokcha River with the Panja River (which flows from the western extremity of Lake Victoria and forms the major headstream of the Amu Darya) as falling wholly and throughout within the northern limits of Afghanistan. They acknowledged this understanding on the northern limits of Afghanistan by exchange of notes in St Petersburg in January 1873.

Britain had friendly relations with Amir Sher Ali of Afghanistan during 1869-73, and it, therefore, felt no need then for any precise definition, survey, and demarcation of Afghanistan's frontiers with Russia (and Bukhara) from the Heri Rud to the Amu Darya. Need for such a definition arose only on the eve of Russia's seizure of Merv in 1884 and Panjdeh in 1885. Russia also established itself in the Zulfiqar Pass in total disregard of the agreement of 1873. Russia's seizure of Panjdeh came as a serious blow to British prestige in

Afghanistan and Central Asia; for Britain had assumed responsibility for the conduct of Afghanistan's foreign relations since the peace treaty signed in Gandamak on 26 May 1879 and had pledged its help to Afghanistan in warding off any aggression on that country. Britain's failure to help on this occasion reinforced the crisis of confidence it had created earlier by annexing Baluchistan and Chitral, which had been feudatories of Afghanistan.

After installing itself at Merv (now Mari) Russia claimed suzerainty over all the territory inhabited or frequented by the Turkmen tribes. The vagueness of the agreement of 1873 with regard to this section of the frontier led to difficulties. For instance, the agreement mentioned only Maimana as falling within the limits of Afghanistan, "the desert beyond belonging to independent tribes of Turkomans". Russia, which wanted to obtain a strategical frontier south of the waterless desert, persistently maintained that the Hindu Kush, north of Chitral, and not the Amu Darya, was ethnologically and geographically the proper boundary between its own Central Asian possessions and Afghanistan. It thus called in question Afghanistan's title to the entire territory of Maimana, Aqchai, Khulm, Shibarghan, Andkhui, Sar-i-pul, Balkh, and Tashqurghan, as well as Badakhshan, Rushan and Shignan beyond the Hindu Kush. Historically, these had been subject alternately to both Afghanistan and Bukhara from time to time.

Following an armed clash between the Afghans and the Russians in Panjdeh in March 1885, Britain and Russia agreed on 10 September 1885 to appoint a joint Afghan-Russian boundary commission (with Britain representing Afghanistan) for the demarcation of the 350-mile long strip between the Heri Rud and the Amu Darya bordering the Turkmen territory. The commission completed the work of demarcation from the sternly beautiful cliffs of the Zulfiqar Pass up to Dukchi in March 1886. The 40-mile strip from Dukchi up to the Amu Darya could not be demarcated owing to differences over the location of a place named Khoja Salih on the Amu, which, according to the agreement of 1873, was the point at which the boundary was to touch. The agreement of 1873 had mentioned Khoja Salih as a "post" on the Amu Darya. Actually, there was no place called Khoja Salih. It was the name of a district which belonged to Bukhara.

The boundary, settled by negotiations and demarcated by erection of pillars in 1887, passed the Zulfiqar Pass on the Heri Rud, Maruchak on the Murghab River (below the crossing of the Kushk

River near Panjdeh), and Kham-i-ab on the Amu Darya.[5] The award gave Panjdeh to Russia and the Zulfiqar Pass to Afghanistan. There was in fact no town named Panjdeh, the nomadic Sarikh tribesmen being scattered up and down the valley in settlements of varying size.

The joint boundary commissioners also went into certain questions such as the question of border irrigation, particularly the use of the water of the Kushk River, as well as the pasture rights of the people on both sides.   Although they established no regular machinery to regulate the common use of border waters as was done later in the Soviet period, what they did is perhaps the first instance of settling such important questions by negotiation and treaty.

This demarcation of the northern boundary of Afghanistan also enabled Britain and Russia to facilitate the travel of Western scholars, men of adventure, and soldiers to Central Asia.   The archaeological explorations and finds of the scholars travelling in the area created widespread interest in Central Asia.   According to their discoveries and researches, the ancient civilizations of Central Asia were of a cosmopolitan character moulded by the play of Persian, Indian, and Chinese influences on the local genius.

The failure to define the Afghan-Russian boundary in the Pamir east of the Sarikol district in 1872-73 had left the passage into India open.   The Russians had then acknowledged the extension of the jurisdiction of Wakhan up to the foot of the Pamir mountains but had later declared it as a sort of no-man's land.   At the time of the Sino-Russian protocol of 1864 also, the Russians had expressed a desire to establish themselves in the Sarikol district, which commanded all the routes between eastern and western Central Asia and gave access to the passses that lead from the Pamir mountains into the upper Indus Valley and Kashmir.   The consequence of the Russian occupation of the Sarikol district could be, in the event of any erosion of the Anglo-Russian understanding regarding Afghanistan, to extend the sphere of Russian dominance up to the frontier line formed by the convergence of the Hindu Kush and Himalaya ranges.   The Treaty of 1864 had authorized Russia to rectify its boundary south of the Tien Shan mountains, whenever conditions of Kashgar permitted, and China could not then have resisted such a move on the part of

[5]A.C. Yate, *England and Russia Face to Face in Asia : Travels with the Afghan Boundary Commission* (Edinburgh and London, 1887), p. 190.

Russia. Subsequent political developments in the Pamir, especially the military collision between Afghan and Russian troops there on 24 June 1892, provide ample supporting evidence in the matter.

The Ishkoman, Baroghil, and Darkot passes, which separate Chitral and Yasin from Wakhan, were strategically important for the British. The Ishkoman Pass, from which one can command the Baroghil Pass as well, provides direct entry into Yasin, and any army crossing the Ishkoman Pass can reach Gilgit in three marches and from there threaten Punjab either by way of Kashmir or *via* Torbela. By taking Kokand in 1874 the Russians had placed themselves almost at the same distance from the Baroghil Pass as the British, whose nearest military post was at Abbotabad in the Hazara district.

The 1892 incident led to strain in the relations between Afghanistan and Russia. The controversy did not terminate until March 1895, when it was agreed that the cis-Amu portion of Darwaz, where the Amu makes its great bend to the north at Ishkashim, should be ceded to Afghanistan and that Afghanistan should evacuate those portions of Rushan and Shignan which lie on the right bank of the Panja River. Despite numerous difficulties, a joint Anglo-Russian Pamir boundary commission demarcated the boundary from Lake Sarikol to the Taghdumbash Pamir and set a definite limit beyond which Russia was not to advance in the direction of India. The Pamir boundary settlement created a new sector of the Afghan-Russian frontier by drawing a line from previously recognized Afghan territory to a point on what both the British and the Russians agreed to recognize as the Chinese frontier.

The British, who had always looked upon the northern and western boundary of Afghanistan as constituting the real frontier of India for defence against aggression by any Power from the north or the west, were never really able to obtain any solid footing in Afghanistan despite continuous diplomatic and military efforts.

Afghanistan, which concluded several treaties with the RSFSR before attaining freedom on 27 May 1919, signed a 12-Article treaty with the RSFSR in Moscow on 28 February 1921. The treaty bound the two countries not to enter into any arrangement with a third Power in any way detrimental to either of them. The Russians also offered (by implication) to hold a plebiscite (*vide* Article 9) in the Panjdeh and Pamir areas to determine whether these should belong to Afghanistan or the RSFSR. The plebiscite thus offered to be held was, however, never carried out.

To prevent any kind of incident from occurring on the Afghan-Soviet frontier and also to settle such incidents as might actually occur, the two Governments agreed, on 13 September 1932, to appoint frontier commissioners, six from each country, and specify their areas of operations.

Several agreements have been reached between Afghanistan and the Soviet Union since the Second World War. Mention may be made, for instance, of the agreement signed in Moscow on 13 June 1946 which redefined the boundary along the Panja River and settled conflicting water claims.[6] The agreement also provided for the incorporation of the Kushk district, ceded to Afghanistan in 1921, into the Soviet Union. It, further, exactly defined the Afghan-Soviet boundary along the *thalweg* (mid-channel) of the Amu Darya and reaffirmed the determination of the two countries to adhere to the boundary line that had separated them before 1917. Lack of precise definition of the geographical location of the islands of Yangi Kila and Urta Tagai in the earlier border treaties had given rise to frequent disputes between Afghanistan and Russia.

This account of Russia's marches with Turkey, Iran, and Afghanistan reveals certain definite patterns in its politics and diplomacy on its southern borders. Russia's general policy towards Turkey, Iran, and Afghanistan has always been to attach and/or draw them to itself. While the Tsarist period affords more instances of the blatant use of military means in both the demarcation of borders and the settlement of border questions, the revolutionary period reflects a greater use of diplomacy for the same purpose. The efforts made by the Soviet Union to regulate and utilize its frontier river and water resources jointly with Turkey, Iran, and Afghanistan on the principle of "equitable apportionment" have helped in keeping down to the minimum the possibilities of its getting involved in disputes with those countries. Taking into account Afghanistan's interests, the Soviet Union agreed in 1946 to move its international frontier with that country from the southern bank of the Amu Darya to its mid-channel in the non-navigable part and thus transferred to Afghanistan a part of what had been Soviet territory. (It did this in conformity with the usual Middle Eastern and West Asian practice to designate the *thalweg,* the line of the deepest depression of the river

---

[6] W.K. Fraser-Tytler, *Afghanistan : A Study of Political Developments in Central Asia* (London, 1950), p. 170.

bed, as the boundary line.)

Since the 1780s, when Russia first advanced its frontiers to the Black Sea and gained the right of free navigation in the Black Sea and passage through the Bosphorus and the Dardanelles, the sea Powers of the West have not wanted the land power of Russia to capture the passage between the Black Sea and the Mediterranean. Britain and France fought Russia in the Crimea in 1854 and narrowly missed doing so again in 1877 in an effort to stop it both from breaking up the Ottoman Empire and from expanding in the Balkans and in Asia Minor. Germany joined Austria, Britain, and France against Russia only after its emergence as a Great Power in world affairs in 1870. The Anglo-Austrian *entente* over the Eastern Question ended in 1879, but Britain and France continued to oppose Russia's claim to Constantinople and the Straits up to 1915 in order to protect the sea routes to the East, especially the Suez Canal, from the menace posed by Russia's increased power.

When Russia started expanding towards Turkey and Persia in the eighteenth century in the first instance, it did not find it easy to conquer those countries outright, and it, therefore, adopted a policy of forcing them to cede some of their northern territories and thus gradually pushing them southwards to their natural confines. It sought, besides, to win over the ruling families in those territories by conferring upon them high-falutin titles in Russia and by appointing them to important military posts within the Russian Empire. With the dawn of the nineteenth century, it followed this policy more aggressively than ever before. The relations that it thus established with Persia and Afghanistan led eventually to serious differences with Britain. Britain incurred the furious hatred of Russia especially after the Berlin Congress of 1878, where it adopted a hostile attitude towards Russia. Russia resolved to punish Britain severely for its hostility by frustrating its designs in West Asia. The British had been apprehending danger to their possessions in India from rival European Powers ever since they learnt of the collusion between the French Emperor Napoleon I and Tipu Sultan of Mysore in the late eighteenth century and their plan for a joint effort to drive the British out of India. Their fears were aggravated by the alliance, forged about this very time, between France and Persia. Of course, Russia had been a Power in Central Asia (from the time of the conquest of Kazan just west of the Caspian Sea in 1552 and the establishment of Orenburg east of the Ural mountains in 1732) long before Britain appeared on the political scene of India. However, from 1894 onwards, Britain and Russia came to terms with each other, and the Anglo-Russian convention of 31 August 1907 set forth their respective spheres of influence in Central Asia and settled their differences in the Middle East and Central Asia. The international boundaries settled by this convention have endured to this day without any significant change, notwithstanding the stresses and strains of the turbulent era that followed.

Turkey, Iran, and Afghanistan on Russia's southern rim are of great economic and strategic importance to both the Soviet Union and the West. Important strategic centres and sources of economic power lie here, among others the Black Sea and the oil wells of Baku. Before the Second World War, Western colonies and empires in South Asia and the spheres of economic interest of the maritime Powers in West Asia, mainly Britain and France, put a solid barrier against the repeated efforts of continental Russia to reach the southern seas. Since the Second World War, important changes have taken place in both West Asia and South Asia, as well as in the balance of power in the Mediterranean area. The West is now endeavouring to build up Turkey and Iran as the strong northern tier against the Soviet Union. It is concentrating especially on Turkey, which has a long history of resistance to Russian advance southwards. Turkey joined the Western defence system—the North Atlantic Treaty Organization (NATO)—on 18 February 1952. The strategic importance of Turkey in the Eastern Mediterranean cannot easily be exaggerated.

The Soviet Union looks upon the NATO as well as the Central Treaty Organization (CENTO) in sharp contrast to its attitude towards the Middle Eastern Pact of 1937, in which even Afghanistan was a participant—as an effort by the West to encircle it in a ring of iron and regards western economic and political interests in Turkey, Iran, and Afghanistan as possible occasions for intervention in its zone of security. These interests also lie in its way to the Mediterranean and the Persian Gulf. It regards the area south of Batum and Baku as the area of its aspirations.

Turkey established diplomatic relations with Russia in 1495, in the wake of its first ever treaty with Poland in 1490. Russia first openly came on the scene as an adversary of Turkey following its alliance with Austria against Turkey in 1696. Since then Russia and Turkey have fought hundreds of battles against each other. One consequence of these encounters was the dissolution of the Ottoman Empire. Turkey's foreign policy continues to regard resistance to Russia's advance southwards as its main objective. In the context of contemporary international politics, Turkey sees, as in the past, an opportunity to secure Western support to stabilize its position and put an effective check to the Russian effort to control the Black Sea. Under the influence of the West, the Turks passionately believe that the Soviet Union is bent on a widening expansion of power by either annexation or domination. The renewal by the Soviet Union of the old Tsarist claim to Ardahan and Kars and the demand made by it for a naval base in the Turkish Straits in 1946 are constant reminders to the Turks of Russia's historical urge to seek an outlet to the southern seas. Soviet Russia can fulfil its ambition only if it secures a stronghold in the Turkish Straits, and any effort that it might make to that end is sure to bring it into conflict with Turkey. A Soviet-Turkish understanding was, is, and will ever remain a historical necessity. Misunderstanding between Turkey and the Soviet Union can lead to dangerous developments both for them and for the world at large. Turkish-Soviet friendship and/or collaboration will greatly strengthen the Soviet Union's position. Unfortunately, the West will never want this to happen.

Since the beginning of the seventeenth century, when Boris Godunov attempted to form with Persia a league against Turkey, the history of the frontier relations between Persia and Russia has been quite fascinating. Despite numerous Russian encroachments upon Persia, including Catherine II's attempt to conquer Persia in the mid 1790's, the Persians have always had strong leanings towards Russia. French effort to unite Persia with Turkey against Russia in 1796 and the British effort to unite Persia with Turkey in the late 1870s ended in utter failure. Turkey and Persia were not only divided by sectarian strife (Sunni vs Shii) but also estranged politically through border disputes, and ever since Sultan Selim's invasion of Persia in 1514 the two countries had drifted apart. Persia perhaps found in Russia a possible counterweight against Turkey. Sectarian hostility played no mean part in the decision of the Shah of Persia not to go to the help of the Sultan of Turkey during his difficulties with Russia in 1877-78. Indeed the Shah went so far as to conclude negotiations with the Tsar during that time for the passage of Russian troops through Persian territory. The prospect of a Russo-Persian alliance is even now a matter of the greatest dread to the Turks.

Russia has kept a close watch over Afghanistan for centuries. Russia's concern has been twofold. First, its moves in the direction of Afghanistan have been the moves of empire-building against the British in India. Second, Russia's frontier with Afghanistan has never been a natural separating barrier such as a mountain range or a large body of water. It has always been the relatively smooth plains of Central Asia. The one great barrier that might serve as its natural border there is the mighty Hindu Kush range, but Russia has never been able to reach it. During the hey-day of empire the British were ever jittery to hear of a Russian mission in Kabul. They started the First Afghan War in 1838 to put an anti-Russian ruler on the throne of Afghanistan. They started the Second Afghan War in 1878 because Kabul had received a Russian mission and rejected a British one. Afghanistan, formerly a British preserve (forbidden to Russia), has been a Russian preserve (forbidden to Britain) since 1921. Right now the presence of the Soviet Union is unmistakable in Afghanistan, and the history of Afghan-Russian relations since the beginning of the nineteenth century shows that the Soviet Union will not easily tolerate any Power, even China, to disturb and/or disregard the present political situation in Afghanistan.

The doings of the Soviet Union have implications, according to the West, for the West Asia and South Asia and especially for Turkey, Iran, and Afghanistan. Russia has never been more imperialistic in West Asia than India was in Afghanistan in the days of the Mughals; or Turkey, Iran, and Afghanistan were in the Caucasus, Central Asia, and North India up to the middle of the eighteenth century; or China is even now in Central Asia and Tibet. Will the Soviet Union, which abandoned imperialism in 1917, now reverse this process and suppress rather than support nationalism in West Asia? It would seem that it has finally turned its back on imperialism. When it rejected China's proposal to re-examine the validity of the present Sino-Soviet boundary, all that it meant to convey was that it was determined to defend the boundaries it had inherited on the eve of the Revolution of 1917.

FIVE

Lamas in Central Asian Politics

Till the Chinese took control of Tibet in the summer of 1951, the Buddhism of Tibet, popularly known as Lamaism, was always a force to be reckoned with in the politics of Central Asia. All adherents of Lamaism looked with reverence upon Lhasa, for it was the most sacred seat of the Dalai Lama, the spiritual and temporal head of Tibet. China's policy towards Tibet, therefore, always took account of the influence of Tibet's high lamas over the peoples of Central Asia and Siberia, especially the Mongols. So did its policy towards states in the Himalaya, such as Bhutan, Sikkim, and Nepal. In 1959, when the Tibetans rose up against Chinese rule, and the Dalai Lama deemed it necessary to leave Tibet and seek political asylum in India, China detained in its custody in Tibet a good many of the leading lamas belonging to the countries in the Himalaya, and especially the lamas of Ladakh, who were all then in residence in the monasteries of Tibet for purposes of study, for possible use in creating trouble in those countries.

The development of Buddhism in the Tibetan environment had earned Tibet the religious leadership not only of the people of Tibetan extraction but of those of the Himalaya, Mongolia, and Siberia as well. This religious leadership was evidenced by the highly complex nature of the relationship that existed between Tibet on the one hand

and China, Mongolia, and the states in the Himalaya on the other. The arrival of Britain and Russia on the political scene of Central Asia made the relationship further complicated. The main concern of British policy towards Tibet, therefore, was to forestall any possible hostility on the part of the controlling influence in Lhasa towards India and the states in the Himalaya. Britain's interests in Tibet were primarily trade and friendly intercourse with the countries in and across the Himalaya, and the cultivation of the high lamas towards the achievement of these ends. Russia's interests in Tibet included not only the strengthening of the loyalty of its Buddhist population in Siberia and the Ural-Volga region but also the spread of its influence beyond its borders in Mongolia, Tibet, and the Himalaya border countries like Nepal. Russia too thus found it necessary to pursue a policy of friendship towards the high lamas of Tibet. Japan's interests in Tibet were to win Mongolian support for itself in Central Asia and to establish a sovereign state of Mongolia within the sphere of its own influence.

The favour of the high lamas of Tibet was thus sought after by several different Powers at the same time. Even the lesser lamas of Tibet were in demand, for they were useful as surveyors, emissaries, and intelligence agents. The high lamas of the countries in the Himalaya, Central Asia, Siberia, and the lower Volga region, who depended on Tibet for religious education and training, always played an important role in shaping the destiny of their peoples and guided their political relations with China, India, and Russia.

THE HIMALAYA

The Gaden Namgyal Gonpa of Tawang in Arunachal Pradesh, the biggest Buddhist foundation in the entire Himalaya from Arunachal Pradesh in the east to Ladakh in the west, belongs to the Gelugpa (commonly referred to as the Yellow Sect because of the yellow hats of its adherents). Down to 1950 it was a subsidiary of the great Drepung Monastery of Lhasa, and its head lama was always chosen from among the abbots of the Drepung Monastery.

The rise of the Gelugpa in the sixteenth and seventeenth centuries and its vigorous proselytizing activities undermined the strongholds of old sects like the Nyingmapa (commonly referred to as the Red Sect because of the red hats of its adherents) and led to migrations south of the Himalaya, especially to Bhutan, Sikkim, and Nepal. In the beginning of the seventeenth century (in 1616 to be precise),

Ngawang Namgyal (1594-1651), a scion of the house of Gya of Drug and Ralung and the head of the Drug subsect of the Kargyudpa, fled to Bhutan. The Kargyudpa sects were then rent with intense jealousies and internal rivalries. Ngawang Namgyal founded in Bhutan the southern branch of the Drugpa, known as the Lho Drugpa, and proclaimed Bhutan a theocracy and himself its supreme head and ruler with the title of *Shabdung*. The descendants of Ngawang Namgyal, like the descendants of the great lamas who had visited Bhutan before 1616, were in course of time regarded as *chhojes* (religious lords).

During his reign of thirty-five years, Ngawang Namgyal unified Bhutan for the first time. For the administration of the religious affairs of the country, he created the office of *Je Khenpo* (Lord Abbot). For the administration of the secular affairs of the country, including Bhutan's relations with the neighbouring countries, he created the office of *Desi* (Regent), known as the Deb Raja in East India and Nepal. He built most of Bhutan's big forts and monasteries like Punakha and Paro. He appointed governors to look after the regions, and district officers to assist them in the administration of the country. He also made a code of laws specially for the protection of the peasants.

Ngawang Namgyal's success against his internal rivals, the representatives of other Kargyud sects and their patrons, as well as against the Tibetans greatly impressed his neighbours. Sengge Namgyal (*r*. 1590-1640), the great king of Ladakh, recognized his spiritual authority and granted him a number of villages around the holy Mount Kailash in Western Tibet to be used for mediation and worship. Down to 1959, a Bhutanese lama, designated *Chila* (Lama Chief), administered those villages with the assistance of a layman.

In 1728-30, a civil war raged in Bhutan over the question of the Shabdung Rinpochhe. The non-ruling Bhutanese faction approached the Tibetans for help, which led to the murder of the then Desi, Wang Paljor, and the confirmation of the disputed incarnation as the Shabdung Rinpochhe. In 1770, the establishment of the Shabdung Rinpochhe staged a *coup d'etat* to depose Shidar, who had, following his appointment as the Desi in 1768, concentrated all power in himself. Raja Prithvinarayan Shah of Nepal, who had just established neighbourly relations with Desi Shidar, refused to recognize the Shabdung Rinpochhe's nominee in place of Shidar.

After the rupture between Nepal and Tibet in 1788, the Svayambhunath Temple in Kathmandu came under the protection of the Shabdung Rinpochhe, who appointed a Chila there. The Bhutanese Chila in Western Tibet also wintered there from time to time.

The later Shabdung Rinpochhes remained very much in the background. The incarnations of the Shabdung Rinpochhe at the time of the Anglo-Bhutanese conflicts of 1838-39 and 1864-65 were minors. The father of the infant Shabdung Rinpochhe tried strenuously in the mid 1830s to protect the status of his ward in the secular affairs of Bhutan. His negotiations with the British in this behalf failed. In the summer of 1864, the establishment of the Shabdung Rinpochhe proposed to the British that they send a fresh envoy, and said that if the British did not find it possible to do so, they would send one themselves. The British Government rejected this proposal on the ground that it was just a subterfuge to gain time. Actually all that the British wanted was an opportunity to inflict punishment on the Bhutanese for their anti-British attitude during the great rebellion in India of 1857.

The institution of Shabdung Rinpochhe in Bhutan, like that of Dalai Lama in Tibet, withered away with the creation of the institution of the hereditary monarchy of Bhutan in 1907. It is, however, important to note that the British thought it necessary from the legal point of view to have the seal of Shabdung Rinpochhe VII (Jigme Dorje, 1905-31), affixed to the Treaty of Punakha of 8 January 1910, which made it obligatory for Bhutan to be guided by the advice of the Government of India in its external relations.

Thus, till the emergence of a hereditary monarchy, Bhutan, like Tibet, was a theocracy. The Shabdung Rinpochhe, the head of the Drukpa Kargyudpa, was the supreme ruler. The lamas were consequently supreme in the government and virtually ran the administration of the country. Although the emergence of the monarchy meant much loss of power for the lamas, the kings of Bhutan have so far been able to keep them in good humour. In 1931, when Shabdung Rinpochhe VII died, there were several claimants to the high office of Shabdung Rinpochhe. No attempt was, however, made to identify and install the reincarnation. One of the claimants to this office is living at present in Himachal Pradesh, and is revered by the Bhutanese and other adherents of the Drugpa Sect in the Himalaya.

The Je Khenpo functions today as the head of Buddhism in Bhutan.

A group of the Nyingmapa lamas, escaping to Sikkim from persecution in Tibet in the mid 1630 (on the eve of the ascendancy of the

Gelugpa to political power in Tibet), introduced Buddhism in Sikkim. In 1641, they installed Phuntsog Namgyal (1604-70) as the first king of Sikkim. In 1705, during the reign of Chagdor Namgyal (r. 1700-16), Jigme Pawo, the last incarnation of Lhatsun Chhenpo Kunsang Namgyal, built the Pemayangtse Monastery. Therefore, the Chabgon Rinpochhe, the head of Pemayangtse (the main monastery of the Nyingmapa in Sikkim, the dominant sect of Sikkim), is the head of Sikkimese Buddhism. He is regarded as the incarnation of Jigme Pawo. He has the privilege of consecrating the ruler of Sikkim on the occasion of his *Gser khri mngah gsol* (enthronement ceremony).

The pioneer lamas exhorted Phuntsog Namgyal to rule the country in a religious spirit. They also gave him the title of *Chhogyal* (King who rules according to the *Chho*, "Righteous Law", and enforces respect for it). Thus the ascendancy of the lamas was established in Sikkim in the very beginning. The high lamas of Sikkim have frequently intervened in temporal affairs. The Chhabgon Rinpochhe took the leading part in the campaign against the settlement of immigrants of Nepalese origin in Sikkim in 1875-85.[1] During the Anglo-Tibetan War in the summer of 1888, he favoured a settlement with the British within the framework of the Anglo-Sikkimese Peace Treaty of 28 March 1861, which had established British paramountcy over Sikkim.

The high lamas of Sikkim have frequently been members of the royal family and the lay upper class. The lama members of the Chhogyal's Council have always been closely related to the ruling class. Reincarnations and leading lamas have always been personages of influence in the country. Several rulers of Sikkim, including the present Chhogyal, also have been high lamas.

Nepal, the starting-point (along with Assam and Kashmir) of the spread of Buddhism to Central Asia, never developed Buddhist institutions of the type prevalent elsewhere in the Himalaya, Central Asia, and Siberia. The various sects of Tibetan Buddhism in Nepal are generally the subsidiaries of those in Tibet.

The high lamas of Spiti, Lahul, and Ladakh never achieved much political power, though they frequently participated in affairs of State of their countries. The mother monasteries of the main monasteries of Arunachal Pradesh, Lahul, Spiti, and Ladakh—like those of Bhutan, Mongolia, Nepal, and Sikkim—have always been in Tibet.

[1] Government of Sikkim, *Sikkim: A Concise Chronicle* (Gangtok, 1963), pp. 11-13.

MONGOLIA

Buddhism, which made an abiding impact on the culture and customs of the Mongol peoples, firmly established itself in Mongolia in the sixteenth century as the State religion. Its head was the Jetsundamba Khutukhtu (in Tibetan, *Rjebtsun dampa hothog thu*, "Lord Incarnate") an object of great faith and veneration for the people of Mongolia. The Jetsundamba had several titles, one of which was *Bogdo Gegen*, "Holy Teacher". Whereas the first two incarnations of the Jetsundamba from 1635 to 1759 appeared among the sons of the princes of the Khalkha Mongols, all subsequent incarnationas appeared in Tibet. This was because, in 1757, Emperor Chi'en-lung forbade the "discovery" of the reincarnations of the Jetsundamba among the Mongols and decreed that these reincarnations should be looked for thereafter only in Tibet. The idea behind this decree was to prevent a family alliance between high leaders in civil and religious life. Jetsundamba II (Lobsang Tenpai Dronme, 1724-59) was a key figure in the Mongol revolt of 1756-57, which posed a serious problem for the Manchus. The Manchus were able to suppress it mainly because they were able to overawe Jetsundamba II in time. His influence would have been decisive if it had been allowed to be exerted on the side of the rebels. The suppression of the rebellion strenghthened the control of the Manchus over the Khalkha Mongols. Thus the rebellion of 1756-57 is a turning-point in modern Mongolian history. Of all the incarnations of the Jetsundamba, the first and the last influenced the life, history, and culture of the people of Mongolia most. Jetsundamba I (Yeshe Dorje *alias* Lobsang Tenpai Gyaltshen, 1635-1724) received the title of Jetsundamba from Dalai Lama V in 1650. He played an important part in the first relations of the Khalkha Mongols with Manchu China and submitted them to the suzerainty of Emperor K'ang-hsi in 1691. During the period 1677-87, when there was an internecine conflict between the Khalkha and Jungar Mongols, a section of the Khalkha princes decided to place themselves under the protection of Russia. Jetsundamba I, the real ruler of the Khalkhas, opposed their decision and persuaded them to drop it, asserting that Buddhism would not be protected in that case and that they ought to place themselves under the protection of China instead.[2]

[2]Charles R. Bawden, *The Jebtsundamba Khutukhtu of Urga* (Wiesbaden, 1961), pp. 5-6.

Thus the Manchu policy of patronizing Buddhism started paying off. In the winter of 1687, Russia sought the good offices of Jetsundamba I in the settlement of the Sino-Russian disputes relating to the Amur border. The Mongols were not yet subject to the sway of China. The conclusion of the Treaty of Peace by China and Russia at Nerchinsk on 7 September 1689 marked the end of the Sino-Russian rivalry over the Mongols.

Jetsundamba II established a theological seminary in the Gaden monastery in Urga. It drew theological students from all over Mongolia and Siberia. As a result, by the late nineteenth century, Urga became a major Buddhist training centre in Siberia.

Jetsundamba VIII (Ngawang Lobsang Chhokyi Nyima Tenzin Wangchuk, 1871-1924) declared the independence of Mongolia from both the Manchus and the Russians, and proclaimed himself monarch and head of the Mongol State on 1 December 1911 during the first Mongol Revolution, which began a little earlier than the Chinese Revolution of the same year. He also assumed the title of *Khan* (King) of the Khalkha Mongols on 28 December 1911. The Jetsundamba declared Mongolia's political separation from China on the ground that it was a vassal state of the Manchu Empire, and that the overthrow of the empire (though the Emperor had not yet abdicated) had in effect severed its political connection with China.

Russia's ambition to bring Mongolia within its own sphere of influence was always great, and it, therefore, signed on 3 November 1912 a 4-Article agreement (and a 17-point protocol annexed thereto) with the Jetsundamba providing for Russian assistance in the maintenance of Mongol autonomy. It gave Russia the right to train Mongolian soldiers and station Russian troops in Urga, the Mongolian capital, denying China the right to station troops there. Mongolia borrowed two million rubles from Russia on the condition that Russian advisers could supervise its finances. It also established a national bank that was in fact run by the Russians. Russia also exchanged notes with China on 5 November 1912 and urged China to accept the Mongolian decision to set up an autonomous state under the leadership of the Jetsundamba but under China's suzerainty. Yuan Shih-kai sent emissaries to Urga to talk to the Mongolian leaders, and sought to convince the senate that it was necessary to accept the Russian conditions concerning Mongolia. He hoped to secure the Mongols' allegiance to the Republic by making concessions to them.

Meanwhile, on 11 January 1913, Mongolia and Tibet concluded a 9-Article treaty in Urga and recognized each other as independent countries. On 17 October 1913, the day Russia recognized the Republic of China, Yuan's regime announced recognition of Mongolia's autonomy. By an agreement to this effect, which China signed with Russia in Peking on 5 November 1913, China accepted Mongol autonomy. By the same agreement, Russia acknowledged China's suzerainty over Mongolia. Heavy pressure from both China and Russia thus reduced Mongolia's independence to mere autonomy under the suzerainty of China.

The Jetsundamba, who did not take kindly to the continuance of the suzerainty of China over Mongolia, put his seal nevertheless, under duress, to the agreement which China and Russia signed with him on this subject in Urga on 7 June 1915. Under extreme pressure from the Chinese (Russia being powerless at this time), the Mongol princes and heads of Government Departments in Urga signed on 16 November 1919 a memorandum announcing their "voluntary" liquidation of Mongol autonomy. The Jetsundamba preferred Japan to China or Russia as overlord. He inspired a strong pan-Mongol movement, rallying it around himself, in the peripheral areas of Mongolia (i.e. Aga, Barga, Shillingol, Kobdo, and Tuva) on the border with China and Russia. Taking advantage of the disturbed political situation in Russia during the civil war following the Bolshevik Revolution, Japan became active in Mongolia. It exploited, though without success, Russian difficulties in Mongolia and Siberia from 1917 to 1921. It helped with money, arms, and officers the anti-Soviet Ungern Sternberg, who drove out the Chinese from Urga in February 1921 and ruled Urga for nearly five months. On 6 July 1921, he was captured by Mongolian and Soviet troops. He was subsequently shot. He had enjoyed Japanese support in his Mongol venture. Japan assisted him in setting up the autonomous Mongol State with the Jetsundamba as the titular head of State and also encouraged him to resist the Bolsheviks in Siberia. Ungern Sternberg in his turn supported the Japanese scheme of a greater Mongolia (comprising both the inner and outer parts, the Barga area of Manchuria west of the Khingan mountains, and the Buryat country east of Lake Baikal) free of Chinese influence.

Circumstances compelled the Jetsundamba to turn to Soviet Russia through the underground Mongol revolutionary leaders in 1920-21. On the establishment of the people's power in Urga following the second Mongol Revolution on 11 July 1921, the Mongolian People's Revolutionary Party (MPRP), which had led the Revolution, decided, in view of the situation then obtaining in the country and the unique social, cultural, and religious proclivities of the Mongol people, to keep the monarchy and let the Jetsundamba, symbol of the old order, continue as head of State with the title of Khan. Of course, the revolutionaries limited his absolute power by requiring his decrees to be countersigned by the new Government controlled by them and by obliging him to pledge non-interference in the decisions of the People's Government. After his death on 20 May 1924, the People's Government issued a decree on 13 June 1924 abolishing the monarchy and disallowing the search for his reincarnation. The Grand Hural, the Mongolian Parliament, met towards the end of 1926 to deliberate whether to abolish or to preserve the position of Jetsundamba in the life and politics of the Republic and, after much discussion, ratified the 1924 decree in the matter. Thus was abolished this powerful, religious institution of the Khalkha Mongols, and the ties with the past were severed.

The news of the official Mongolian decree disallowing the search for the reincarnation of the Jetsundamba greatly shocked the people of Tibet. A year prior to his passing away Dalai Lama XIII even mentioned it as a warning in his political testament to his own people: "Unless we now learn how to protect our land, the upholders of the Buddhist Faith, the glorious incarnations, all will go under and disappear and leave not a trace behind....All beings will suffer great hardship and pass their days and nights slowly in a reign of terror." However, the high lamas of Tibet searched for the reincarnation of the Jetsundamba. This reincarnation is now living, as a refuge, in the Darjeeling hills.

The Government of the Mongolian People's Republic discovered the value of Buddhism in the field of cultural diplomacy after the emergence of sovereign states in South-East Asia. It revitalized the dormant institution of *Hambo Lama* (in Tibetan, *Khenpo Lama*) of the historic Ganden Monastery (first built in 1838 during the time of Jetsundamba V, 1815-40) in the capital of the Republic. The Hambo Lama has, in his capacity as the President of the Mongolian Buddhists' Association, participated in the biennial general conferences of the World Fellowship of Buddhists since 1956, the year of the 2,500th Buddha anniversary. In summer 1969, he took the initiative in organizing the Asian Buddhist Council and in holding under its auspices the Buddhist leaders' conference on Vietnam and Peace in the summer of 1970. Later, he also organized an institute for the training of lamas from Mongolia and the Soviet Union. An important activist in the Mongolian peace campaign, his endeavour is to promote peace through Buddhism.

How anomalous this revival of the Mongolian interest in Buddhism, which had become outdated for both the Mongols and their Government with the passing away of the Jetsundamba Khutukhtu in 1924 !

RUSSIA

The several Buryat tribes of the Lake Baikal region of Siberia, the northernmost of the Mongol peoples, received their Buddhism (in the form of Lamaism) directly from Tibet. Russia pursued a two-pronged policy towards these ancient people of the Baikal region. On the one hand, it encouraged the spread of Christianity among them, and, on the other, it sought, by making Buddhism legal in 1752, to take advantage of the attachment of their feudal hierarchy to Buddhism. A decree of Tsarina Elizabeth in 1741 made the head lama of the Tsongol monasteries the head of all the Buryat lamas. Another decree of Tsarina Catherine II (the Great, r. 1762-96) on Lamaism in Eastern Siberia in 1767 combined the title of *Bandido* (in Sanskrit, Pandita) of the head lama of the Selengge monasteries and the title of *Hambo* (in Tibetan, *Khenpo*) of the head lama of the Tsongol monasteries to form a new title, *Buryat un Shasin u ejen Bandido Hambo Lama* (Bandido Hambo Lama of the Buryat Buddhist Order), and conferred it on the head lama of the Tsongol monasteries. Yet another decree in 1809 said that the head lama of the Tsongol monasteries should take up residence in the monastery of Guzino Ozero, the Buryat cultural and religious centre. In 1812, the Bandido Hambo Lama received high commendation from Moscow for prayers for victories over the enemy. On 15 May 1853, Russia reaffirmed the 1767 decree. The Office of Examiner for Religious Affairs (Moscow) and the Office of the Selengge Tribes (Irkutsk), first established in 1807, regulated and supervised all affairs of the high lamas in Siberia up to 1917.[3]

The Torgut Mongols, who had migrated westward from the Chuguchak/Tarbagatai frontier area (in the course of a long struggle

---

[3]B. Rinchen, *Four Mongolian Historical Records* (New Delhi, 1959), pp. 129 and 145.

with the Chinese) to the pasture lands between the Ural and Volga rivers in 1630, kept their politico-religious connection with Tibet. This helped them in 1771 to return to the Ili Valley, their former homeland in Central Asia, following the limitation of their autonomy by Catherine II. Their Hambo Lama appealed to Dalai Lama VIII to set a propitious date for the commencement of their journey "home". Russia set up the Office of Kalmuk Tribes (Astrakhan) for the administration of such Torguts as had remained behind in the Volga delta. Interference by the local lamas in the civil affairs of the Kalmuks led to the passing of strict laws against them through their Hambo Lama in 1838. Up to 1917, however, the Hambo Lama's role as the head of Buddhism in the Ural-Volga region remained important, and the Kalmuk Mongols continued to look up to the Dalai Lama for advice and guidance. The Bolshevik Revolution changed it all. The Dalai Lama, who had all along had retainers among the Kalmuks, was deprived of his time-honoured prerogative to sanction the appointment of the Hambo Lama. In 1929, on the occasion of the third conference of Soviet Buddhists (their first and second conferences had been held in 1923 and 1926 respectively), when the Kalmuks elected their Hambo Lama (1929-45), the Soviet regime had already decided that no religion, not even the Buddhism of the Kalmuks, should be allowed to flourish on Soviet soil.

When Lama Jaya Yin (1711-77), the first Buryat to receive his religious education in Lhasa from 1725 to 1740, went to Moscow as a deputy in 1767, he carried letters and presents from Dalai Lama VII to Catherine II. This was the first time that such letters and presents had ever passed between a Dalai Lama and a Russian monarch. P.A. Badmaev (1851-1919), a Buryat doctor (of the Tibetan system) of medicine, who had a lucrative practice in St Petersburg and who was a functionary of the Asiatic Department of the Ministry of Foreign Affairs, asserted, in a memorandum to Tsar Aleksander III in January 1893, the desirability of extending the great Siberian railway complex from Lake Baikal to Kansu in China, next to Tibet. He even offered to engineer there, with the help of the Buryat lamas resident in the leading Gelugpa monasteries, the annexation of Tibet to Russia. Badmaev's idea attracted the attention of Count Sergei Yulgevich Witte, Russia's Finance Minister from 1892 to 1903, who saw in it the extension of Russian influence southward into Tibet and the Himalaya border countries like Nepal, quite in accordance with the then Russian policy of expansion in East Asia.

Agvan Dorjiev (in Tibetan: Ngawang Dorje, 1849-1938), a Buryat lama who was a confidant and adviser of Dalai Lama XIII, played an important part in this regard. He appears to have impressed the Dalai Lama with the Tsar's earnest interest in the promotion of Buddhism in Siberia, and especially with the idea of the Tsar as the Protector of Buddhism. He gave currency to the beliefs that the Tsar was the *Kalki avatar* and that the idyllic country of Shambhala described in the folklore of Tibet and the literature of Tibetan mysticism was no other than Russia, and, what is more, he was able to sell these ideas to the credulous Tibetans. Significantly, on the occasion of his visits to Livadia and St Petersburg on behalf of the Dalai Lama in 1898, 1899, and 1901, he was received by Tsar Nikolas II (1894-1917), the Tsarina, Count Witte, and others. He accompanied the Dalai Lama in his flight to Urga on the eve of the advance of the British military expedition to Lhasa in the middle of August 1904. He advised the Tsar on all problems relating to Buddhism in Siberia, Mongolia, and Tibet. On the establishment of Mongol autonomy in 1911, he represented the Dalai Lama in Urga, and arranged a treaty of alliance between Mongolia and Tibet. Like the great Buryats Mikhail Bogdanov (1879-1919) and Ts. Z. Jamtsarano (1880-1940), he played a leading role in Mongolian politics from 1900 to 1928, and worked incessantly for the rise of a greater Mongolia. Like Bogdanov, he visited the geographically remoter Kalmuks in 1905, and founded in the town of Burgutse a religious school for the education of Kalmuk Buddhist youth.

Naturally Britain could not view the Russian advance towards Tibet and the Himalaya with equanimity. Lord Curzon, then Viceroy and Governor-General of India, sent a military expedition to Tibet in 1903-4 to put an end to Russian intrigue there. For a long time the British mistook for Russians the Tsar's Buryat subjects who visited Tibet, Nepal, and India on pilgrimage, and regarded Agvan Dorjiev as an arch spy for the Tsar. Their worst suspicions were roused when in 1901 Dalai Lama sent a mission under the leadership of Agvan Dorjiev to the Tsar of Russia. The checkmating of Russsia's moves in Tibet, therefore, became the principal concern of the British policy towards Tibet.

Russia feared that British expansion in Tibet might increase Britain's prestige in Central Asia and influence Russia's Buddhist subjects. It, therefore, could not remain indifferent to any disturbance of the *status quo* in Tibet. It was not then continguous (as indeed it is not even now) with Tibet, but most of its Buryat, Tuvinian, and Kalmuk subjects, being adherents of the Gelug Sect, regarded the Dalai Lama as their leader and looked up to him for advice. Russia was thus naturally anxious to prevent any hostile influence from being established in Lhasa.

The Soviet leaders were at first inclined to use Buddhism as a bridge between the Communist and non-Communist worlds. They even conceived of a big role for the Buryat Buddhists, particularly for Agvan Dorjiev, who was then head of Buddhism in Soviet Russia and who had once played an important part in the history of Central Asia (especially as an intermediary between Tsar Nikolas II and Dalai Lama XIII). They thought that they could be of considerable help to them in converting all the Buddhists of the world to communism. Indeed Agvan Dorjiev and leading Buryats such as Jamtsarano declared that Buddhism was actually a religion of atheism, that there was no difference between the Buddhist ideas about the emancipation of mankind and the ideas professed by Karl Marx and Vladimir Lenin, and that Buddhism was in fact the forerunner of the materialism of communism. The Congress of Soviet Buddhists held in Moscow in January 1926, arranged mostly by the Buryat intelligentsia, appealed to the Buddhists of Mongolia, Tibet, and India to support the Chinese people in their crisis in 1926-27. After 1929, however, there was a change in the Soviet attitude towards Agvan Dorjiev's role as a religious leader. They even suspected him of being a Japanese agent, and officially described his theories regarding Buddhism as harmful.

Nevertheless, on the eve of the Second World War, Buddhism among the Buryats was still a factor that the Communist Party of the Soviet Union (CPSU) had to reckon with. The high Buryat lamas still had considerable influence with the masses. The Soviet leaders realized that they could ill afford to belittle the role of Buddhism in Asian politics, and revived the institution of Bandido Hambo Lama. Since 1956, the Bandido Hambo Lama, in his capacity as the President of the Soviet Buddhists Association, participates in the biennial general conferences of the World Fellowship of Buddhists. He frequently goes to Moscow, from his distant headquarters in Ulan Ude, to act as host to distinguished Buddhist visitors from South-East Asia to the Soviet Union. He is also an important activist in the Soviet peace campaign, and participates in the conferences of the World Peace Council. The present Bandido Hambo Lama, J.D. Gombo-yin (1897-   ), who was consecrated in 1963, visited Sikkim on a goodwill mission soon after his installation.   He also led a three-member delegation of Soviet Buddhists to the International Inter-Religious Symposium on Peace held in New Delhi from 10 January to 14 January 1968.   His endeavour is to promote peace through Buddhism.

CHINA

The monks of Kubilai Khan (r. 1280-95), who made Lamaism the national religion of the Mongols, played a unique role in Mongol politics and diplomacy in Europe.   All this made it easy for the Mongols to exercise control over the Tibetans without actually invading and occupying their country.   Chinggis Khan (1167-1227) was the first to bring Tibet under Mongol control in 1206.   The expansion of Chinese influence in Tibet dates only from the conversion of his grandson Kubilai Khan to Buddhism in the second half of the thirteenth century, giving Buddhism and Buddhist monks in Tibet unique power and prestige.

The Mings (1368-1644) continued the Mongol policy of patronizing the high lamas to serve the imperial interests beyond the Great Wall of China.   They were able by sheer diplomacy to maintain their supremacy in Tibet.   The old sects of Tibetan Buddhism were then engaged in a struggle with one another for ascendancy in both temporal and religious spheres.   The Mings deemed it politic to raise the Kadampa and Kargyudpa hierarchs to equal rank with the Sakya hierarch, encouraged strife among them, and thus broke the power of the great lama of Sakya.   Whereas the Mongols gave primacy to the Sakya Monastery above others, the Mings extended their patronage to the main monasteries of all the other sects, and thus made sure that no particular monastery or sect rose to a position of preeminence. Altan Khan of Tumed Mongols embraced Buddhism and created the institution of Dalai Lama in 1578.   His example was followed by large number of his people.   This mass conversion in the sixteenth century was encouraged by China.

The Manchu rulers of China (1644-1911) were quick to appreciate the importance of the hierarchs of the Gelug Sect in any policy towards Central Asia.   Their policy was to use Buddhism to tame the Mongols and to soften their military spirit.   This policy, according to the 1793 decree of Chienlung on Lamaism (which is inscribed in the Chinese, Manchu, Mongol, and Tibetan languages on the Yung-ho-kung Temple in Peking), necessitated its protection in the tradition of the Mongol and Ming dynasties: "As the Yellow Church inside and outside [of China proper] is under the supreme rule of those two men [Dalai Lama and Panchen Lama], all the Mongol tribes bear allegiance to them. By patronizing the Yellow Church we maintain peace among the Mongols...."[4]

In appreciation of the assistance given by the high lamas of Tibet in ensuring their control over the Mongols, especially their spiritual leaders, the Manchu rulers bestowed on them religious gifts, honours, ranks, and titles and exempted the Tibetans from all compulsory levies and services of the State. The early Manchu rulers established lama dignitaries and erected places of worship even in Peking and Jehol. They even constructed palaces modelled on the Potala of Lhasa. K'ang-hsi called the religious dignitary of the Amdo country to Peking in 1693, designated him Teacher of the Empire, bestowed on him the dignity and title of *Changkya Khutukhtu* after his village, and installed him in the Yung-ho-kung as his religious representative in Mongolia. In 1696-97, he delegated Changkya Khutukhtu I (Ngawang Lobsang Chodan, 1642-1714) to go to Lhasa and convey gifts on his behalf to Dalai Lama VI, who had ascended the throne a little time before, and to Panchhen Lama II (Lobsang Yeshe Palsangpo, 1663-1737) and other high lamas of Tibet. Emperor Yung-cheng (1722-35) sent Changkya Khutukhtu II (Yeshe Tenpai Dronme *alias* Rolpai Dorje, 1717-86), along with Kengze Chin-wang (the seventeenth son of Emperor K'ang-hsi, who was a patron of Buddhism), to accompany Dalai Lama VII during his return from exile and to witness his reinstallation in Lhasa in 1734. (The situation in Tibet was in the firm control of Pholhane, and there was now little to be gained by keeping the Dalai Lama and his father out of Lhasa.) Changkya Khutukhtu II took his final vows and received the name Yeshe Tenpai Dronme from the aged Panchhen Lama II when he visited Tashilhunpo towards the end of 1735. He helped to pacify, through his influence with Jetsundamba II, a rebellion in Khalkha which had developed from the trial of Chingunjav, the brother of Jetsundamba II. Changkya Khutukhtu II again went to Lhasa in 1758 after the death of Dalai Lama VII to supervise the succession. He also ordained Jetsundamba III (1759-73) and bestowed on him the name of Yeshe Tenpai Nyima. In 1781, he initiated Jetsundamba IV (Lobsang Thubten Wangchuk Jigme Gyamtsho, 1775-1813). Dalai Lama XI

---

[4]F.D. Lessing, *Yung-ho-kung* (Stockholm, 1942), vol. 1, pp. 58-61.

was enthroned in the Potala in the presence of the Changkya Khutu-khtu on 25 May 1842.   In the first year of the Republic of China, the then Changkya Khutukhtu went to Mongolia, as the emissary of Yuan Shih-kai (Provisional President of the Republic), to persuade the Mongols not to sever their political connection with the new regime in China.   The Republic nominated him honorary President of the Commission for Mongol and Tibetan Affairs.   The present Changkya Khutukhtu, the sixth in the line, is in Formosa.

The Changkya Khutukhtus always played important roles in the selection of the grand lamas of the Mongols, including those in Siberia. The Changkya Khutukhtus presided over the Yung-ho-kung printing establishment, which had the exclusive right to publish polyglot editions, especially those of the Kangyur and Tangyur codices.   The Yung-ho-kung later became the residence of the Dalai Lama's representative in China.

K'ang-hsi took special interest in the religio-political affairs of Tibet, not so much because he regarded Tibet as a country of strategic importance for him as because he wanted to prevent a coalition between the powerful Jungar Mongols of Ili and the Gelugpa hierarchs of Tibet; for a Mongol-Tibetan alliance could seriously affect the loyalty of the Mongols on China's western border with Russia.   The Manchu conflict with the Jungars was a serious matter, for the Jungars had created the last of the great nomad empires of Central Asia, and they had established their sway from the Great Wall in the east to the Caspian Sea in the west. This bitter Manchu-Jungar conflict, which dominated the history of Central Asia during the first half of the eighteenth century, largely influenced Manchu policy towards Tibet, especially from 1707 to 1757, and made the Manchus seek a *rapprochement* with the Dalai Lama.   Russia, which had conquered the Ob-Yenisei region and which could not tolerate the challenge of the Jungars for long, had already emerged supreme in its rivalry with the Jungars.   Ironically, in 1727, Tshewang Rabdan (*r.* 1697-1727), the man who consolidated the empire of the Jungars, died at the hands of his own lamas who thought that in accomplishing his destruction they were avenging the havoc wrought by the Jungar army in Tibet in 1717.

Patronage of the high lamas of Tibet always enabled the Manchu rulers of China to govern, fairly effectively, the wild inner Asian frontier region, especially Tibet and Mongolia, without any expensive occupying army.   The Tibetans and the Mongols worshipped the

Buddha and had implicit faith in their lamas. The Manchu patronage of Buddhism and the lamas was thus in accordance with their Central Asian policy. From a spiritual point of view, the Manchus were no admirers of the lamas. Their interest in patronizing Buddhism or in helping the spread of its influence among the Mongols is to be ascribed to their appreciation of Buddhism as a political instrument in the subjugation and control of Mongolia and Tibet.

Kuomintang advisers, particularly Wu Chung-hsin, who was chairman of the Commission for Mongolian and Tibetan Affairs from 1938 to 1942, and Professor Li An-che, a cultural anthropologist and one of China's foremost experts on Tibet, advocated the exercise of influence in Tibet mainly through the support of the principal hierarchs of the Yellow Sect. The Kuomintang programme of cash endowments to various powerful Yellow Sect monasteries such as Sera, Drepung, and Ganden (near Lhasa) and Tashilhunpo (near Shigatse) for the purpose of entertaining lamas there was helpful in the extension of Chinese influence in the monasteries. This created a feeling that the Chinese were of the same religion after all, and countered the opinion of those Tibetans who had been in China that Buddhism was little venerated there and that in their attitude towards Buddhism in Tibet, as in much else, the Chinese were not sincere. This policy of maintaining the power of the hierarchs of the Yellow Sect, vigorously advocated by Professor Li before and after 1949, enabled the People's Liberation Army to gain its first foothold in North-Eastern Tibet in the winter of 1950.

The Government of the People's Republic of China felt it both expedient and politics not to disturb the *status quo* in the land of the lamas. On 23 May 1951, it drew up a 17-point agreement in Peking, and secured the approval of the representatives of the Government of Tibet. This agreement, which sought to legalize and regulate the "peaceful liberation" of Tibet, provided for the maintenance of the "status, functions, and powers" of the Dalai Lama and the Panchhen Lama.

In 1956, during his visit to India in connection with the 2,500th Buddha anniversary celebrations, the Dalai Lama asked for asylum. It was only after receiving certain assurances from the Government of the People's Republic of China through Jawaharlal Nehru, Prime Minister of India, in respect of the implementation of the terms of the 17-point agreement of 1951 that he allowed himself to be persuaded to withdraw his request for asylum and return to Tibet. The rebellion of the people of the Amdo and Kham regions in Eastern Tibet in 1957, and the refusal of the request of the Chinese military commander in Lhasa to the Dalai Lama to help suppress it in 1958, eventually led, on 10 March 1959, to the great but abortive uprising of Lhasa. Of course, the invitation extended by the Chinese authorities to the Dalai Lama to visit their military camp and the Tibetan interpretation of it as an attempt on their part to kidnap him served as the immediate cause of the uprising. On 11 March, the Government of Tibet denounced the 1951 agreement with China. The Dalai Lama fled Lhasa on 17 March, crossing over to India on 31 March. This flight of the Dalai Lama, the bulwark of resistance to the rapid Sinification of Tibet, marked the end of Tibet's autonomy and its buffer position between China and India. However, Panchhen Lama VII (Thinle Lhundub Chhokyi Gyaltshen, 1938-), confrere of Dalai Lama XVI stayed on in Tibet. Although he dissociated himself from the rebellion of Lhasa, his refusal to accept the chairmanship of the Preparatory Committee in place of the Dalai Lama, especially his refusal to denounce the Dalai Lama in 1963, caused a rift between him and the Chinese. Subsequently, the Chinese deposed and denigrated the Panchhen Lama, a key figure in Sino-Tibetan politics. It is doubtful if he is still alive. The flight of the Dalai Lama created reverberations even in lands as far-off as Burma and Sri Lanka (countries most friendly to China then) where Buddhist monks openly called for the repudiation by their respective countries of the policy of peaceful coexistence with China.

Britain was never able to develop for itself a position similar to that enjoyed by China in Tibet. To cultivate the friendship of Panchhen Lama III (Lobsang Palden Yeshe, 1738-80), Warren Hastings, Governor-General of the English East India Company from 1772 to 1785, established a lama temple on the right bank of the Hooghli near Calcutta in 1775. The British also invited Panchhen Lama VI to India during the visit of the then Prince of Wales (later King George V) in 1905-6. Being fully familiar with the kind of game that China had always played in Tibet, they insisted, during the British-Chinese-Tibetan tripartite conference in Simla on the question of Tibet in 1913-14, that the selection and installation of the Dalai Lama should remain entirely within the competence and control of the Government of Tibet.

Japan and Russia, on the other hand, occupied a unique position in Tibet. Through their subjects, the Mongols, they had direct entry into Tibet and exercised great influence on the powerful Yellow Sect monasteries and through them on their patrons, the men of affairs. To placate the Mongols and the Tibetans and especially the Buddhists in Siberia after the victory of Japan over Russia, Tsar Nikolas II established a lama temple in St Petersburg in 1907 with the blessings of Dalai Lama XIII through the agency of Agvan Dorjiev. Japan on its part organized a Japanese-Mongolian Buddhist Association in Japan in 1918 to win support for its policy towards the Mongols.

The high lamas of Tibet, who neither impressed the rulers of New China nor inspired them towards any objective but that of subjugation, are now all fallen. So is Dorje Phagmo, abbess of the great Samding Monastery in Central Tibet. Neither her miraculous powers, which, it is said, enabled a former incarnation of this grand abbess to save Samding from desecration by the Jungar soldiers in 1717, nor the body-guard allowed to her by the Government of Tibet as a religious pre-rogative, could deter the personnel of the People's Liberation Army of China from carrying out their orders. It is ironical that the lamas, who once played a prominent role in the history and politics of Central Asia, who always offered strong resistance to despotic autho-rity in Tibet, and who were able, in their heyday, to deny Tibet all intercourse with the rest of the world, have now themselves been denied any contact with the outside world by Tibet's present rulers. In any case, the dominance of the lamas over the political thinking of the Tibetans and over the Government and the affairs of Tibet could not have lasted much longer under the changing conditions in Tibet, and in the countries bordering Tibet, especially China and India.

SIX

Mullahs in Central Asian Politics

Wherever Islam went, it made a profound impact on the life and politics of the peoples it touched. Till the Chinese took over Eastern Turkistan in 1949, the mullahs of Islam were strong force in the politics of Central Asia. Their prestige among the Muslims from the Great Wall of China in the east to the Crimea in the west was a political consideration which no regime in China or Russia had ever even been able to overlook, especially after Russia's advance towards Turkey, Persia, and Afghanistan in the seventeenth and eighteenth centuries. The Sultans of Ottoman Turkey often sent them as their emissaries to Persia, India, and Afghanistan to stir up anti-British insurrections in Egypt and India and anti-Russian trouble in the Caucasus and Central Asia. The Mughal Emperors of India also used them as their emissaries to Central Asia, Persia, Russia, and Turkey. Both the Manchu Emperors of China and the Tsars of Russia availed themselves of their services in the pacification of the nomadic tribes of Central Asia and Siberia. Britain, Germany, and Japan engaged them to promote and secure their respective interests in the Caucasus, Central Asia, and India. The British intrigued with the mullahs of Central Asia during the Russian Civil War of 1918-20, which sought to nip in the bud the Bolshevik Revolution there. The British, the Germans, and the Japanese played on the religious sentiment of the people of the

Muslim republics of the Soviet Union and urged them to unite against the "godless Soviet", to secede from it, and to establish sovereign independent Muslim states. Even today the mullahs are being used by the People's Republic of China and the Soviet Union, especially in their cultural diplomacy and peace campaign in Asia and Africa. The United States of America also has been increasingly interested in Central Asian mullahs in recent years.

This chapter deals with the mullahs in the politics of the main area of Central Asia between the Great Wall of China in the east and the Caspian Sea in the west. It does not, however, include *all* the Muslim areas of China and the Soviet Union from the Pacific to the Crimea; it does not even cover the southern fringes of Central Asia. It does not consider religious movements which rebelled against the establishment and resorted to violence in the countries concerned. Owing to the position of the ruler of the Ottoman Empire both as the Khalifa (or the supreme religious head of the faithful of the entire Muslim world), and as the Sultan (or the supreme political head of the only existing Muslim Empire since the end of the Mughal rule in India in the eighteenth century), it starts by assessing the political role of the mullahs of Turkey up to the laicization of that country in the mid 1920s. It then goes on to assess the political role of the mullahs of other countries such as Russia and China. It also deals with the manner in which Japan, though a non-Muslim country, sought to use the mullahs in its grand designs in Central Asia, especially after the battle of Mukden in 1905, when it emerged as a Great Power with a stake in the mainland of Asia.

TURKEY

Ottoman Turkey played an indisputably important part not only in the consolidation of Islam as a religion but also in the politics of the countries where the Muslims resided. The idea of the Ottoman Khalifat as the pan-Islamic political movement largely developed under Sultan Abdul Aziz (*r.* 1861-76). Apart from granting political asylum to those Muslims from India who had participated in the independence rebellion of 1857 under the leadership of Shahzada Sultan Ibrahim, who had close connections with the Nizam of Hyderabad (Deccan), and Firoz Shah, who was a direct descendant of Bahadur Shah I, Sultan Abdul Aziz made them liberal grants (in the form of stipends) and encouraged them to maintain regular contacts with India through correspondence and pilgrimages to

Mecca and Medina.[1] He established the *Hind Tekesi* (Monastery
of the Darvishes of India) in Constantinople (Istanbul, since
the early 1920s)—the religious centre of the Muslim world. Abdul
Hamid (*r.* 1876-1909) was the first Ottoman Sultan fully to use it
for his own ends, to secure his and his dynasty's state. All great and
small Powers in Asia and Europe sought his favour and goodwill.
Kaiser William of Germany cultivated Abdul Hamid with a view
to befriending the Muslim world and thus bullying Britain, France,
and Russia—each of whom had millions of Muslim subjects—into
an accommodating mood.

The Shaikh-ul-Islam, chief Mufti of Constantinople and chief
of Islam chosen by the Ottoman Sultan himself directly from the
ulema (the entire body of Muslim doctors of theology), was the high
priest of the Ottoman Empire. He was the head of the religious
side of the Ottoman Empire, and constituted, along with the Ministry
of Religious Affairs, the final authority on the *sheriat,* the sacred law
of Islam and the supreme law of the Ottoman Empire. His supremacy in this field always enabled him effectively to influence the secular affairs of the Ottoman Empire. Mehmet II (*r.* 1808-39), the
greatest of the Ottoman Sultans, created in 1826 the office (later,
Ministry) of *Ewkaf* (Religious Endowments) and the office of
Fetwaname (Issuance of Religious Decrees) and made the office
Shaikh-ul-Islam an integral part of the State machinery.

To depose the Sultan, the Commander of the Faithful, it was necessary to secure the sanction of the Shaikh-ul-Islam. It was indis-
pensable to obtain the blessings of the Shaikh-ul-Islam in any move
to depose the Sultan, and his disapproval was tantamount to a veto.[2]
The Turkish sociologist, Zia Gok Alp, according to the memorandum
submitted by him to the Congress of the Committee of Union and
Progress (the Young Turks up to 1906) in the autumn of 1917, advocated the abolition of this office as a part of the religious reforms to
be introduced in Turkey.

The Shaikh-ul-Islam sent emissaries to China in 1907 to establish
the Khalifa's spiritual connection with the faithful of Islam in those
remote parts. Raja Mahendra Pratap of the Indian Revolutionary

---

[1]Albert Howe Lybyer, *The Government of the Ottoman Empire in
the Time of Suleiman the Magnificent* (Cambridge, Mass., 1913), pp.
207-15.

[2]Mahendra Pratap, *My Life Story of Fifty-five Years* (Dehra Dun, 1947),
pp. 44-45.

Committee in Berlin, set up in 1951 after the outbreak of the First World War, had a series of audiences with the Khalifa, Sultan Rishad, and the Shaikh-ul-Islam, Hairi Effendi, in the summer of 1915 in the course of his mission to Afghanistan to seek the advice of Amir Habibullah of Afghanistan on the steps needed to liberate India from the British yoke, to get in touch with the Indian revolutionaries there, and to carry anti-British propaganda into India.[3]

The pan-Islamic and pan-Turkic propaganda during the First World War to unite the Muslims and the Turks had considerable effect in Central Asia, Persia, Afghanistan, and India. It also influenced events in the Caucasus in 1917. The Allies were at this time losing heavily to the Central Powers in Europe. The Russians, unable to stand up to the advancing Austrian, German, and Turkish armies, were withdrawing from the Caucasus and Persia. General Nuri Pasha made no secret of his intention to march an "army of Islam" through the Caucasus to the Caspian Sea and beyond to seize Azerbaijan and the Caspian coast of Persia, rally the Muslims of the Caucasus and Central Asia, and threaten India. This was perfectly in line with Turkey's pan-Turkic ambitions and Germany's plans against the British in Afghanistan and on the North-West Frontier of India, where the tribes were already giving trouble to the British. The success of the German plans could seriously affect the loyalty of the Muslims in the Punjab and the North-West Frontier, on which the army of British India had always drawn heavily for reinforcements.

The Turkish question was intimately connected with the Indian problem. The European plan for the dismemberment of the Ottoman Empire was a cause of acute anxiety to most Indian Muslims, who looked upon the Ottoman Sultan as the head of Islam uniting in his person both spiritual and temporal power and hence as their religious leader. When the conflict between Ottoman Turkey and the Balkan states came to a head in the winter of 1912, the British Government was very reluctant to exert any pressure on Ottoman Turkey for fear of the possible repercussions of any such step on its part in India. Indeed it was obliged to disregard public opinion in Britain itself, which had manifested the greatest enthusiasm for the principle of "the Balkans for the Balkan people", and resort to a *volte face*. It, however, tried to control the Khalifa and thus assume the leadership of the Muslim world.

[3]A.H. Brun, *Troublous Times : Experiences in Bolshevik Russia and Turkestan* (London, 1927), pp. 103-4.

On its defeat in the war of 1914-18, Ottoman Turkey stood shorn of its imperial possessions in Europe and Asia alike. Both Britain and France divided its Asiatic possessions between themselves as mandatories. (The British occupied Constantinople on 16 March 1920). In accordance with the terms of the armistice, Greece received Thrace. This greatly enraged the Indian Muslims, who vehemently resented the breach of peace terms, especially the British pledges to maintain intact the Ottoman Khilafat, and they went so far as to start a movement, called the Khilafat movement, in India in February 1920 in order to restore the territorial authority of the Ottoman Sultan as the Khalifa. The movement raged for two years and more, shook the very foundations of the British Empire in India, made the Indian Muslims politically aware and active, and revolutionized the outlook of the people of India as a whole. Under the advice of Mahatma Gandhi, who had then just emerged as the leader of the Indian National Congress, it called upon the people to boycott British goods, resign from Government services, repudiate Government titles, and so on. To support the Khilafatists the Indian National Congress launched a non-cooperation campaign. The joint Khilafat-Non-cooperation agitation assumed tremendous dimensions. Thousands of Muslims, including Leftist intellectuals of the nationalist movement, left the Punjab on what they called *hijrat* (self-exile to escape religious persecution) for Afghanistan, Central Asia, and Turkey. This they did in deference to the mullahs, who had proclaimed British India a *dar-ul-harb* (abode of war or enemy country), and had issued a *fetwa* to the effect that it was an act of sin to continue to live under an anti-Islamic Government. (Thus the Hijrat movement was an offshoot of the Khilafat movement.) Many of those who thus migrated and who came to be known as *muhajirin* (Muslims in self-exile) later turned to the Communist Party of India founded by M.N. Roy at Tashkent on 17 October 1920. These muhajirin were, however, never permitted to enter Turkey, which distrusted them. After receiving training from the Bolsheviks in Moscow and Tashkent, many of them returned to India to organize the freedom struggle against British imperialism. The British Government tried many of them in a long series of the so-called *Bolshevik Conspiracy* (meant "to deprive the King-Emperor of his sovereignty over India") cases in Peshawar, Lahore, Kanpur, and Meerut during 1922-33. M.A. Ansari, as President of the All India Khilafat Committee, even called for the formation of an Asian federation in 1922.   All this happened by way of protest against the British oppression in India.   The Khilafat agitation in India ended only with the conclusion of peace by Britain with Turkey in the summer of 1923.

On 1 November 1922, the *Turkiye Buyuk Millet Mejlisi* (Turkish Grand National Assembly) separated the Sultanate (representing temporal power) from the Khilafat (representing spiritual power) and abolished the Sultanate.   It, however, retained the high office of Khalifa, but with the reservation that it would be open only to those of the house of Osman (1258-1326), leader of the Kayi Khan Turks, who were called Ottomans after him.   Sultan Mehmet VI (Vahidettin *r.* 1918-22), surnamed the "Terror of the World", whose word had been law and before whose whim millions had trembled, fled, a frightened old man, at the moment of crisis.   He left Constantinople on board the British battleship *H.M.S. Malaya* on 17 November 1922.   Next day, the Grand National Assembly elected Abdul Mejid, his cousin and heir apparent, as Khalifa.   Abdul Mejid signed a document pledging to abide by the decisions of the National Assembly.

The spiritual Khilafat was of short duration.   Towards the end of 1923, it was found that Abdul Mejid, who was not unpopular at first with the leaders of New Turkey, did not faithfully follow the conditions under which he had been elevated to the office of Khalifa.   In January 1924, he called upon the dignitaries of the Turkish Republic to clarify his position and powers.   (Turkey had become a republic on 30 October 1923.)   This made Mustafa Kemal Ataturk (1881-1938), the first President of the Turkish Republic, suspend the Khilafat on 3 March 1924 and declare in the National Assembly: "Dignity of the Caliphate can have no other importance for us than that of an historical memory.   The demands of the Caliph that the dignitaries of the Turkish Republic should enter into negotiations with him constitute a flagrant violation of the independence of the Republic." The Aga Khan, leader of the Khoja Muslims, and Ameer Ali, a prominent Muslim leader of India, jointly pleaded for the retention of the Khilafat with its age-old traditions, but succeeded only in hastening the abolition of the Khilafat.   The last Khalifa of Islam, who left Turkey on 4 March 1924 with a son, a daughter, and two wives, sought refuge in Switzerland.   Kemal Ataturk regarded the attempt made by the Aga Khan and Ameer Ali to intercede on behalf of the Khalifa as unwelcome foreign intervention in Turkey's domestic affairs. He disbanded the Ministry of Religious Affairs, proscribed religious orders, abolished the Ministry of Religious Endowments, and ordered religious estates to be sold or otherwise used for the public good. (The Ministry of Religious Endowments had under its control no less than two-thirds of the whole of the arable land of the Ottoman Empire.) The red Ottoman *fez* was outlawed. The mullahs were forbidden to wear their clerical clothes outside the mosques, and a similar prohibition was imposed on the representatives of other religions as well. Even the sheriat was abolished. The abolition of the Khilafat also included the abolition of the historic office of Shaikh-ul-Islam, the administrative organ of the Khalifa. The abolition of the Khilafat was one of Kemal Ataturk's most remarkable achievements. It is divertingly ironical to recall that the movement to defend it had been of great political service to him in his early days. The abolition of both the Sultanate in 1922 and the Khilafat in 1924, as well as the cultural bases that sustained them, were absolute measures in the consolidation of the Republican regime.

The separation of religion and politics in Turkey and the abolition of the Khilafat shook the mullahs of Iran out of their complacency. In Iran also there had been much talk of the possibility of a republic being established with Reza (who had staged the *coup d'etat* of 1921) as its first President. In order to secure their own power, therefore, the Shii religious leaders supported gladly and with alacrity, Reza's ambition to found a new dynasty of his own and continue the ancient institution of imperial monarchy.

RUSSIA

Islam is the second most important religion in the Soviet Union. The Tatar Muslims of the Lower Volga region were the first among the Muslim peoples to encounter the Russians in the middle of the sixteenth century. Among them there developed, in the late nineteenth century, one of the world's main centres of Muslim modernism. It is fascinating to study the relations maintained by the various Governments of Russia with the Muslims of Russia, and the constant shift of emphasis in these relations resulting from considerations of domestic and foreign policies and State ideologies from the time that Russia first subdued the Muslim Khanates of Kazan (1552) and Astrakhan (1554) to the time when Soviet policy succeeded in establishing Russian influence in the Arab world. Until the time of Catherine II, Russia's relations with the Muslims remained largely

negative.   In 1784, she established the Muslim Spiritual Department
in Orenburg.   Central Asia was not yet a part of the Russian Empire.
Catherine did not relish the idea of her Muslim subjects continuing
to look to Bukhara and Ottoman Turkey for inspiration in religious
matters and for instruction in Islamic law and traditions.   The
contributions of the famed social, cultural, and religious institutions
of Bukhara, as of those of Khiva and Kokand to a lesser extent, to the
development of Islamic culture, especially theology, were unique.
So much so that Bukhara was commonly and popularly called
Bukhara-i-Sharif (Holy Bukhara or Bukhara the Holy).

Catherine II was also the first Russian ruler to think of converting
the Kazak and Siberian tribes to Islam through the mullahs of Kazan
—the centre of Islam in Russia—in order to undermine the influence of the mullahs of Bukhara, one of the main centres of Islamic
culture.

The Mufti of Orenburg was the supreme head of the Muslims of
the Ural-Volga region and of Siberia, including the Muslims who
lived in large cities like Moscow and St Petersburg.   The Muslim
Spiritual Department in Orenburg was an arm of the Administration,
and the Mufti was nominated from among the most loyal sections of
the ulema by the Minister for Internal Affairs himself.   The headquarters of the Department was later transferred to Ufa, a town
founded in 1586 at the southern foot of the Ural mountains, near the
confluence of the Belaia and Ufa rivers.   The Russians have always
been conscious of the political consequence of encroaching upon,
or rather of seeming to encroach upon, the traditional customs and
observances of the Muslims.

The mullahs by and large—of course not all of them, and there were
a few notable exceptions—took a leading part in the many rebellions
that occurred in Soviet Central Asia during 1917-27 (which, it is sometimes alleged in certain quarters, were often provoked by the Bolsheviks themselves in their search for an excuse for loot and plunder).
They incited the people against Lenin's decree on land, which established land tenure and private ownership of land throughout the
country and made land national property no longer subject to purchase and sale.   The rebellion was formidable enough to force the
Soviet Government in 1918 to amend some of the basic principles
in the decree on land in keeping with the specific conditions then
obtaining in Turkistan in particular and in Central Asia in general.

Early in July 1918, the mullahs inspired a revolt in Transcaspia against the Tashkent Soviet. Indeed they both abetted and co-operated with the imperialist intervention in the Caucasus and Transcaspia. In September 1920, Mullah Oraz Khoja Muhammed and Mullah Nur Muhammed Babi, along with Baba Akhund Salim, signed, as plenipotentiaries of the Soviet Republic of Khiva, a treaty of alliance and an economic agreement with the plenipotentiaries of the Russian Socialist Federated Soviet Republic (RSFSR) in Moscow. The mullahs of Bukhara participated in the Basmachi movement in the Ferghana Valley, the Pamir, and elsewhere during 1921-22. According to Soviet historians, the mullahs who resisted the Bolsheviks in Central Asia, the Caucasus, and Siberia were reactionaries and agents of the imperialists headed by Britain.

The main aim of Soviet policy towards the Muslims in the Caucasus and Central Asia in the early years was to break up and eliminate the dangerous pan-Turkic ideas and movements advocated by men like Enver Pasha (1881-1922). However, despite the efforts of the Soviet authorities, one such movement, the Basmachi movement, survived, although in a subdued form, up to the Second World War.

During and after the Second World War the Soviet Government followed a relatively soft policy towards Islam. The Muslims of the Soviet Union responded by extending their whole-hearted cooperation in the war effort. An All-Union Congress of Soviet Muslims held at Ufa, capital of the Bashkir Autonomous Soviet Republic, in June 1942 called upon Muslims everywhere to help defeat Nazism. About this time for the administration of Muslim religious affairs, the Soviet Government set up four councils, one each (1) in Ufa for the Muslims of the RSFSR, including Siberia, (2) in Tashkent for the Muslims of Central Asia and Kazakhstan, (3) in Baku for the Muslims of the Transcaucasus, and (4) in Buinak for the Muslims of Northern Caucasus and Daghestan. The councils at Ufa, Tashkent, and Buinak are each headed by a chairman known as **Mufti,** and they look after the religious affairs of the Muslims of the Sunni persuasion generally. The chief of the Muslims of the Shii persuasion in Azerbaijan has the designation of Shaikh-ul-Islam, and he heads the council at Baku. There is a chief for all the Muslims of the Soviet Union, known as the Grand Mufti. His seat is also at Ufa. As in Ottoman Turkey, only men of the best reputation for knowledge of religious matters are said to be eligible for appointment to these high offices. The functions of the councils are, among other things, the administration of all religious affairs, the education and training of future religious leaders, the construction and maintenance of religious buildings and monuments, and the publication of religious books.

The Soviet Government depends on the Mufti of Tashkent for its propaganda among the Sunni Muslims of India and Afghanistan, and on the Shaikh-ul-Islam of Baku for its propaganda among the Shii Muslims of Iran and Iraq. The heads of all these councils are members of the Peace Defence Committee in their respective areas. On such occasions as the conferences of All Churches and Religious Associations for the Defence of Peace held in Zagorsk in May 1952 and July 1969, representatives of the four Muslim councils would address their co-religionists in the Muslim world and declare their commitment to peace in the world. The 1952 conference condemned the United States for its actions in the Korean War. The Soviet delegation to the conference of Asian countries held in New Delhi from 6 April to 10 April 1953 included Ziauddin Babakhanov (assistant to his father, Ibnul Mejid Khan, elected Mufti in December 1942), whose inaugural Arabic speech gave delight to all the delegates, particularly to those of the Arab countries.

Since the 20th Congress of the CPSU of 1956, the Soviet Government has actively, and in recent years successfully, engaged in improving its relations with the Muslim countries of South and West Asia. It now realizes the need for adopting a positive attitude towards Islam both inside and outside its territories. In 1966 it held a most significant conference in Moscow to consider "the Influence of Religion on the Social Thought of the Peoples of the East." This conference found that the importance of religion in the shaping of social and political behaviour had been underrated and any serious study of it neglected. It recognized that Islam in particular had played a great role and recommended the establishment of centres of Islamic studies in Soviet universities.

Islam, which is a way of life, not just a code of beliefs, is by no means dead in Soviet Central Asia, despite the preaching of the mullahs of the post-revolutionary years that Marxism and Leninism were in accord with the teachings of Islam. The social and cultural values of Islam and their influence are an abiding factor in the lives of the Muslims of Soviet Central Asia. Of course, the authorities are still engaged in an effort to supplant the way of life represented by Islam by the one that is represented by communism. Soviet organizations such as the Society for the Propagation of Political and Scientific Knowledge continue to publish anti-religious literature, now called "scientific atheistic propaganda", in order to weaken the grip of religion on the people.

JAPAN

Japan became anxious, for the first time after the battle of Mukden, to secure allies among the discontented Muslim subjects of the Tsar. The Khazaks and the Tatars, who had emigrated from Russia to Japan after the First World War and the Bolshevik Revolution, organized an Islamic cultural centre in Tokyo in 1923 and a Turco-Tatar Society in Kobe in 1934. The Japanese authorities, who regarded the 1934 Congress as important, sent representatives to it. They also brought delegates from Manchukuo to participate in it. On this occasion the Kuran was translated into Japanese for the first time. The Turco-Tatar Society established a school, a publishing house, and a magazine for the spread of Islam in Japan. Thus Japan established rapport with Islam and declared itself the liberator of the Muslim countries.[4] Early in the 1930s, Japan, like Germany and Italy, declared itself the "Protector" of Islam and provoked anti-Muslim incidents in Sinkiang, and other parts of China. These incidents roused the indignation of all Muslim countries, especially Afghanistan and Persia, against China. The Japanese forced the Muslim organizations of China to send delegations to these countries to explain that, in reality, China had no Muslim problem and that, even if it had one, it was not Japan's making. In 1938, they supported the alliance of the five Ma brothers of China, whose principal aim was the unification of all the Muslims of China.

CHINA

Islam spread to China in the eighth century. The *Imam* (head) of the main mosque in Peking has ever since been the spiritual head of all the Muslims of China. Islam first began to matter in the politics of Central Asia only in the early thirteenth century, when Chinggis Khan, after consolidating his empire, breaking the bastions of the 405-mile-long Great Wall of China, and conquering North China and Peking, turned his attention to Central Asia specially to punish an old enemy, Kuchluk. Kuchluk was heir to the throne of the Naiman (Turkic) tribe. He had fled in 1204 and received asylum in 1208 in the court of another of Chinggis Khan's enemies, Yelu Cheluku,

---

[4]Jean-Paul Roux, *L'islam en Asie* (Paris, 1958), pp. 277-8.

last sovereign of the Kara Khhitai Empire (1128-1211). Later he had revolted against his protector Yelu Cheluku, taken him prisoner, and seized the throne. Once on the throne he had started persecuting Islam, the religion of the majority in Kashgar, Khotan, Yarkand, etc. He had even put to death the Shaikh-ul-Islam of Khotan and had greatly harassed the people. When the hordes of Chinggis Khan swooped upon his capital, the people of Kashgar, Yarkand, and Khotan, who were hostile to Kuchluk, welcomed the invaders as liberators. Jebe, the great general of Chinggis Khan, not only put an end to the persecution of Islam but formally authorized the practice of Islam. This enabled him eventually to conquer all the territories that had formed part of the Karakhitai Empire.

Eastern Turkistan, which the Manchus conquered between 1755 and 1757, has had a turbulent history. The mullahs always played a great role in the politics of Eastern Turkistan in the nineteenth and twentieth centuries. The many rebellions that occurred in the first half of the nineteenth century, particularly those of 1825 and 1827, culminated in the overthrow of Manchu rule and the establishment of an independent regime in Kashgar. The Muslim revolt of 1861 spread to Eastern Turkistan from Kansu and Shensi in 1863. Yakub Beg (1820-77) of Kokand in Western Turkistan conquered Eastern Turkistan in January 1865. The Muslims massacred all the Chinese and Manchus resident in Ili, Kulja, and Tihwa (now Urumchi) but spared those who adopted Islam. It took China as many as fifteen years to put down the rebellion. Peace returned to Eastern Turkistan only in 1878. After suppressing the Muslim revolt of the 1860s, China established frontier posts in the region of the Sarikol range to prevent hostile persons from Hunza and Kokand from crossing into Sinkiang and helping the mullahs in creating trouble for it there. The Muslims attempted to get rid of the intruding Chinese troops again in 1930-31, when the Uigur Khoja Niyaz proclaimed the East Turkistan Republic in Kashgar in November 1933, with himself as President and Mullah Sabit as Premier. China put down the Muslim rebels with the help of ammunition received from the Soviet Union by 1934.

The importance of this Muslim uprising is second only to that of 1864-68. Both these uprisings had much to do with the increasing Russian (and Soviet) influence in Eastern Turkistan. Interestingly, on both occasions it was only with Russian (and Soviet) intervention that China succeeded in suppressing the Muslim challenge.

The People's Republic of China vigorously encouraged Islam by establishing mosques in Shanghai, Peking, Nanking, Lanchow, and Hanchow, and by repairing many famous mosques in the country. It also sent Chinese Muslim students for religious education in the famous Al-Azhar University in Cario. All this was no doubt due to the anxiety of the Government to impress foreign visitors with the measure of religious freedom that it allowed to its citizens in spite of being a Communist regime. It was also by way of fulfilling the promise made by Mao Tse-tung in the mid 1930s to the Muslims of North-West China that in the event of their standing by the Communist cause he would ensure that the Communist regime he was trying to set up would give them full religious freedom, protect their distinctive culture, and exert itself to secure the unification of the Muslims of China and Russia. As an earnest of this promise, Mao had even built a mosque in Yenan, his headquarters in those years.

On the occasion of the Peace Conference of the Asian and Pacific Regions held in Peking on 18 October 1952, Burhan Shahidi of the *Chungkuo Islam Djemiyeti* (China Islamic Association), established in May 1953, addressed delegates from the various Muslim countries. The stress placed on Arabic was important from the point of view of the Arab countries. The Chinese delegation to the first Afro-Asian Conference held in Bandung from 18 April 1955 included Mullah Nur Muhammad, Vice-Chairman of the Chungkuo Islam Djemiyeti and a prominent Muslim leader of People's China. The inclusion of this Muslim leader was obviously to impress the Muslims in Asia and Africa, especially the Muslims of South-East Asia, and to assure them of the support and friendliness of the intentions of the Government of People's Republic of China. Premier Chou En-lai, head of the Chinese delegation to this Conference, expressed the hope that "those with religious belief will also respect those without" and underlined the significance of religion in international diplomacy.

China's policy today is to obliterate Islam from China even as it has obliterated Buddhism and Christianity. The Muslims of China, especially those of the Sinkiang-Uigur Autonomous Region, which borders directly on the Soviet Union and where the national minorities like the Kazak and the Uigur outnumber the Han, are full of resentment against the Chinese authorities for seeking to obliterate their religious and social practices and annihilate their native heritage. A crisis in the frontier town of Inin and Kulja, caused by the reallocation of food supplies to other parts of China in May 1962, developed into the last major Muslim revolt against the Chinese regime.

Thousands of Muslims who participated in the revolt were forced to flee over the border to the Soviet Union.

The Chinese Government none the less continues its practice of receiving and sending Islamic friendship delegations. It sent one such delegation, under the auspices of the China Islamic Association, to Iraq, the Sudan, and other Muslim countries in West Asia in 1966. This is mainly to achieve the goodwill of the Governments and peoples of Islamic countries by leading them to believe that the Chinese people, including Muslims, are free to practise their faith. The Chinese Government pretends that there is no repression of Islam in China. Even the Imams, including the Imam of the main mosque in Peking, who have been attacked or disgraced, have been attacked for the ostensible reason that they were anti-national agents of the imperialists and not because they were Muslims.

AFGHANISTAN

Afghanistan, like Turkey, is an Islamic country. Islam has always been a most powerful force in the life of the Afghans ever since its introduction in their country. Its mullahs have always wielded great influence in its politics. The mullahs have had a particularly pervading influence in the economics, politics and society of Afghanistan since its establishment as a modern state by Ahmad Shah Abdali in 1747. The sentiment of Islamic brotherhood cherished by the people of Afghanistan has been far and away the most important factor in the conduct of its foreign relations. No Afghan ruler could stay in power without the approval and support of the mullahs. Even so formidable a ruler as Abdur Rahman (r. 1880-1901) could not afford to disregard it.

Dost Mohammad (r. 1826-63) played on this sentiment when he assumed the title of *Amir-ul-Mominin* (King of Believers) and declared a *jihad* (holy war) against the Sikhs. Abdur Rahman sought to impress both the mullahs and the people that he was not only the temporal head of the nation but also the defender of the Islamic faith. He tried to curtail the powers of the mullahs. He converted the Kafirs of Kafiristan to Islam. The people gave him the title of *Zia ul millat wa din* (Light of the Nation and the Faith). Habibullah (r. 1901-19), who was most eager to open up and develop his country, engaged a number of experts such as teachers, physicians, and engineers, especially Sunni Muslims from India and Turkey. Certain mullahs of the Laghman district accused him of heresy. He hanged a number of them. He also made a tour of the country to explain to his people that his policy was identical with that of his father.

Amanullah (r. 1919-29), who succeeded Habibullah after his murder in 1919, could not flout the popular demand for an Islamic policy in view of the religious sentiment of the people. This enabled him to support the Amir of Bukhara, Enver Pasha, and the Basmachis against Soviet Russia in Central Asia and to protect the rights of the Muslims living in Turkistan and in Bukhara and Khiva. Also on the basis of their common Islamic heritage he sought to forge closer links with Iran and Turkey. Turkey particularly impressed him, so much so that he decided to emulate Mustafa Kemal Ataturk in his plans to transform Afghan society. The mullahs, always jealous of their power and prestige and opposed to any change that might threaten their position, incited the people against his "blasphemous" and "heretic" activities, created a wave of disaffection among the people and frustrated his programme of modernization. The rebellion of Khost in Paktia in 1924, spearheaded by Mullah Gird, was one such manifestation of their fanaticism. In this rebellion, Afghanistan paid dearly in terms of both material goods and human suffering. The mullahs particularly resented Amanullah's fiat enjoining all native visitors to Kabul to wear Western dress and his decree on the education of girls. His move to abolish the custom among women of wearing the *chadri* (veil) also created much ill-will not only among the mullahs but also among high military officers. Bacha Saqqao, who succeeded Amanullah after his flight from the country in 1929 and who was supported by the mullahs, reversed all the reforms introduced by Amanullah. When Nadir Shah took over in 1929, he also undid a number of social reforms introduced by Amanullah. To appease the Islamic sentiment of the people, he adopted a policy of gradual reform.

King Mohammad Zahir (r. 1931-) has been quite successful in his efforts to build the Afghan nation and modernize the country. He has also been able to keep the mullahs in good humour. The mullahs on their part support King Mohammad Zahir's policies of social change and reform in view of the march of time and with the hope that they would thus be able to maintain their influence among the people.

Up to 1917, the mullahs played a significant role in Central Asian politics. They were a force to be reckoned with in the region because of the intimate relationship that obtained then between religion and politics and the immense influence the two together exerted on the life of the people. However, with the intensification of the process of modernization and secularization, their influence began to decline. The separation of politics from religion undermined their power and prestige. At first the Governments of the region, in their over-enthusiasm to do away with the mullahs, took strong measures to eliminate their influence from political life. However, they soon found that the mullahs were too well entrenched in the life of the people of Central Asia to be eliminated summarily. They also realized that they could be utilized to further their national interest, particularly in improving their relations with the countries of the Muslim world. The result was that they adopted a realistic approach and evolved a new role for them: they set them to work as an instrument in the furtherance of the national policies of their countries. There is, however, no question of the mullahs regaining all the power and prestige that they once enjoyed in Central Asia.

SEVEN

Postscript

Central Asia has always been an important area of our world, both historically and politically. From the earliest times China, India, and Iran took active interest in the life and politics of Central Asia. In later times countries like Britain, Japan, and Russia also appeared on the scene.

Till the first century A.D. the primary concern of China's policy towards Central Asia was to keep the nomadic northern "barbarians" outside the Great Wall. Indeed it was this concern which had made the Chinese build the Great Wall for defence against invasions from the north and for the protection of their social structure in the Hwang Ho basin, the "rice bowl" of China. China retreated from Central Asia after the emergence of Islam and the rise of Muslim power in the area during the years 751-90 and did not reappear on the scene till 1949-51. The sporadic attempts it made in the intervening period to reestablish its influence and power were not a great success. Sovereign independent India's relations with Central Asia, and especially with Tibet, had different aspects, but it was the political and cultural aspects that stood out. When India accepted China's claim to Tibet as an integral part of itself, it snapped its political connection with Central Asia. Iran, which suffered its first set-back beyond its natural northern confines with the emergence of Russia in the Caucasus and

Central Asia in the sixteenth and seventeenth centuries, retreated from there during the years 1813-69. Britain was enabled by its position in India to be the only rival of Russia for centuries, even a contender for supremacy for a time, in Central Asia. Japan, which had been nursing an ambition to secure a lasting foothold in Central Asia since the time that the Japanese General Hideyoshi Toyotomi first thought of Japan's expansion on the mainland via Korea in the 1590s, never had much luck. Russia has been a Power in Central Asia since the time it conquered the Muslim kingdom of Kazan in 1552 and crossed the Ural mountains into Central Asia in 1604. The Russian Revolution of 1917 is a landmark in the life, culture, and politics of Central Asia; for the progress material and spiritual, achieved by most of Central Asia during the revolutionary Soviet period is not only spectacular but also profound.

The Mongols were the first to unite Central Asia under one sovereignty. The Turks, who followed them, almost, but not quite, repeated the performance. Although it is they who inhabit most of Central Asia today, any effort on their part to bring the area under one rule on the basis of either pan-Islamism or pan-Turkism seems to be foredoomed to failure.

China and the Soviet Union between them now possess most of Central Asia. Afghanistan and Mongolia are the only two Central Asian states which lie outside their territorial limits. China controls entire Eastern Central Asia. The Soviet Union controls entire Western Central Asia. Whereas the Soviet Union consolidated its position in its part long ago, China has still to secure its position in its part. Whether it will be able to do so remains to be seen. However, the two are now actively contending for primacy there. China is not only claiming territories in Soviet Central Asia, as also in Far East, but also trying to secure the secession of the Soviet Central Asian republics from the Soviet Union thereby destroying the structure, the very basis, of the Soviet Union—a Union of peoples of many races and creeds. Not only has China now crossed the man-made Great Wall and ventured into the lands of the "barbarians", but it has also essayed the great walls erected by nature itself—the Altai, Himalaya, and other mountain ranges in Central Asia. This has created a deep misunderstanding between it and its great neighbours, India and the Soviet Union. Its conflict with the latter has many dimensions to it and profound implications for all mankind. For this conflict for primacy between the two Great Powers in Central

Asia may result in a great cataclysm.

In 1969, China and the Soviet Union unsuccessfully attempted to separate their inter-state relations from their inter-party relations. Of course, ever since Chou En-lai and Alexei Kosygin conferred at Peking airport on 11 September 1969, the two countries have kept their border conflict under control and have taken care not to let it develop into a conflagration. No doubt the Chinese are now better equipped to cope with a Soviet threat than in 1968-69 inasmuch as they have deployed a dozen or more nuclear-tipped intermediate ballistic missiles capable of hitting Moscow and other Soviet cities. Also, they have significantly improved their relations with the United States and Japan. It does not, however, follow that they are anxious to test the nerve and strength of the Soviet Union. They know that the penalty they had suffered for provoking the Soviet Union was fairly stiff in 1969. There had been a debate then in Moscow on the desirability of a pre-emptive strike to cripple China's still limited nuclear capability. Fortunately saner counsels prevailed, and the adventure was never undertaken. Any fresh attempt on the part of China to bait the Russian bear might provoke a harsher and more ruthless retaliation.

China may, therefore, think of other alternatives which do not mean a direct confrontation with the Soviet Union. It may, for instance, create situations elsewhere—say, the region of the northern Pacific Ocean, which is of equal concern to China, Japan, the United States, and the Soviet Union—just to involve the Soviet Union in a wasting warfare and thus to bring about its discomfiture, dissipation of its resources, or defeat. This may later enable China to secure an overall settlement with the Soviet Union.

The failure of the effort made by China and the Soviet Union during 1969-72 to de-escalate the border dispute between them reinforced a change that had already become manifest during the preceding few years in international diplomacy. This change was the change in the pattern of relations between China, the Soviet Union, and the United States. With the Chinese saying that the Soviet Union was their arch enemy, or enemy number one, and American experts speculating that the Soviet Union would make a pre-emptive nuclear strike against China, it was inevitable that China and the United States should draw closer, each to the other. Despite all the bilateral differences between them, and despite their separate obligations to third parties, Peking and Washington have been drawn together by their mutual opposition to Moscow. In order to contain the power of the Soviet Union, a fundamental objective of US foreign policy since the Second World War, the United States has not hesitated to take measures towards normalizing its relations with China, a country which it suspects and hates as much as, if not more, than the Soviet Union. This can have the most profound impact on the rearrangement, currently in progress, of the world's political forces. An alliance between China and the United States, plus Japan, against the Soviet Union also has implications not only for the Soviet Union but for world peace.

It is, of course, true that the change in the American policy denoted by the steps taken by President Richard Nixon to arrive at some sort of an understanding with China is in its own interest. But then there is as yet no indication of any significant let-up in US antagonism towards China. There is also no evidence—not even a rumour—of the United States having offered China an alignment which it could employ against the Soviet Union. Further, in its own interest the United States cannot quit its commitments in the region of the Pacific Ocean. This points clearly to the possibility of a shift of the theatre of conflict between the Great Powers concerned. However, the terror in which these Powers hold each other rules out a direct military conflict between them. They may turn to wars by proxy for pursuing their own goals of hegemony.

Historically Russia (and the Soviet Union) had always felt uneasy whenever some other Power emerged strong or established its presence in Manchuria and the region of the Pacific Ocean. It is not, therefore, surprising that since about the beginning of this century, when Japan emerged as a Pacific Power, it has constantly suspected Japanese motivations and objectives. This suspicion was fed from time to time by what Japan did in the area during the past seventy years—its war with Tsarist Russia (1904-5), its occupation of Siberia (1918-22), its incursions into Mongolia and the Soviet Union (1936-39), and so on. The Soviet Union now seems to feel that although the moves made in mid 1972 towards a normalization of relations between China and Japan are good in themselves, certain recent trends in the relations between those two countries may not be salutary from the viewpoint of its own security. It is afraid that failing to assert its own individuality in the political field, Japan may find itself one day a mere tool of China, which would like to use Japan to further its own ends, especially those which run counter to Soviet interests.

Several recent statements made in the Diet show that the Japanese want to press their territorial claims against the Soviet Union. Perhaps China has promoted the Japanese to demand that the Soviet Union return the Kurile Islands. There are also reports that China agreed during the Sino-Japanese summit meeting in September 1972 that it might give military assistance to Japan in the event of the latter being attacked by the Soviet Union. Japan's reluctance to consolidate its ties with the Soviet Union, especially to sign the peace treaty, has also deepened Soviet suspicions. Perhaps this will lead to a conflict. Hopefully, it may not; for the different contending Powers may find themselves tantalizingly neutralized. That would mean an indefinite, although uneasy, continuance of the present political structure of Central Asia.

APPENDIXES

Appendix I

Chinese-Mongolian Agreement on Economic and Cultural Cooperation, 1952

ARTICLE I

Both contracting parties agree to establish, develop and strengthen cooperation in the economic and cultural spheres and in the sphere of education between the Chinese People's Republic and the Mongolian People's Republic.

ARTICLE II

On the basis of the present agreement and with the aim of implementing it, concrete agreements will be signed separately between agencies of the Chinese People's Republic and the Mongolian People's Republic concerned with questions of economics, trade, culture and education.

ARTICLE III

The present agreement must be ratified within the shortest possible period and will enter into force on the day of its ratification. The present agreement will remain in force for ten years. The exchange of instruments of ratification will take place in Ulan Bator.

If neither of the contracting parties declares its wish to denounce the agreement a year before its expiration, it will be automatically extended for another ten years.

Concluded in Peking on 4 October 1952 in two copies, each of which was drawn up in the Chinese and Mongolian languages. The agreement's texts have equal force in both languages.

> CHOU EN-LAI
> *Premier of the State Administration Council and Minister of Foreign Affairs of the Central People's Government of the People's Republic of China*

> YU TSEDENBAL
> *Prime Minister of the Mongolian People's Republic*

Agreement between China and India on Trade and Intercourse between the Tibet Region of China and India, 1954

The Central People's Government of the People's Republic of China and the Government of the Republic of India;

Being desirous of promoting trade and cultural intercourse between the Tibet Region of China and India and of facilitating pilgrimage and travel by the people of China and India;

Have resolved to enter into the present agreement based on the following principles:

(1) Mutual respect for each other's territorial integrity and sovereignty;

(2) Mutual non-aggression;

(3) Mutual non-interference in each other's internal affairs;

(4) Equality and mutual benefit; and

(5) Peaceful co-existence.

And for this purpose have appointed as their respective plenipotentiaries:

The Government of the Republic of India, H.E. NEDYAM

RAGHAVAN, Ambassador Extraordinary and Plenipotentiary of India accredited to the People's Republic of China, the Central People's Government of the People's Republic of China, H.E. CHANG HAN-FU, Vice-Minister of Foreign Affairs of the Central People's Government, who, having examined each other's credentials and finding them in good and due form, have agreed upon the following:

ARTICLE I

The High Contracting Parties mutually agree to establish trade agencies:

(I)   The Government of India agrees that the Government of China may establish trade agencies at New Delhi, Calcutta and Kalimpong.

(II)   The Government of China agrees that the Government of India may establish trade agencies at Yatung, Gyantse and Gartok.

The trade agencies of both parties shall be accorded the same status and same treatment.   The trade agents of both parties shall enjoy freedom from arrest while exercising their functions, and shall enjoy in respect of themselves, their wives and children who are dependent on them for their livelihood freedom from search.

The trade agencies of both parties shall enjoy the privileges and immunities for couriers, mailbags and communications in code.

ARTICLE II

The High Contracting Parties agree that traders of both countries known to be customarily and specifically engaged in trade between the Tibet Region of China and India may trade at the following places:

(1)   The Government of China agree to specify (1) Yatung, (2) Gyantse and (3) Phari as markets for trade; the Government of India agree that trade may be carried on in India including places like (1) Kalimpong, (2) Siliguri and (3) Calcutta, according to customary practice.

(2)   The Government of China agree to specify (1) Gartok, (2) Pulanchung (Taklakot), (3) Gyanima-Khargo, (4) Gyanima-Chakra, (5) Ranura, (6) Dongbra, (7) Puling-Sumdo, (8) Nabra, (9) Shangtse and (10) Tashigong as markets for trade; the Government of India agree that in future when in accordance with the development and need of trade between the Ari district of the Tibet Region of China and India, it has become necessary to specify markets for trade in the corresponding district in India adjacent to the Ari district of the Tibet Region of China, it will be prepared to consider on the basis of

equality and reciprocity to do so.

ARTICLE III

The High Contracting Parties agree that pilgrimages by religious believers of the two countries shall be carried on in accordance with the following provisions:

(1) Pilgrims from India of Lamaist, Hindu and Buddhist faiths may visit Kang Rimpoche (Kailash) and Mavam Ts (Manasarowar) in the Tibet Region of China in accordance with custom.

(2) Pilgrims from the Tibet Region of China of Lamaist and Buddhist faiths may visit Banaras, Sarnath, Gaya and Sanchi in India in accordance with custom.

(3) Pilgrims customarily visiting Lhasa may continue to do so in accordance with custom.

ARTICLE IV

Traders and pilgrims of both countries may travel by the following passes and route: (1) Shipki La Pass, (2) Mana Pass, (3) Niti Pass, (4) Kungri Bingri Pass, (5) Darma Pass, and (6) Lipu Lekh Pass.

Also the customary route leading to Tashigong along the valley of Shangatsanpu (Indus) river may continue to be traversed in accordance with custom.

ARTICLE V

For travelling across borders, the high contracting parties agree that diplomatic personnel, officials and nationals of the two countries shall hold passports issued by their own respective countries and visaed by the other party except as provided in paragraphs 1, 2, 3, and 4 of this article.

(1) Traders of both countries known to be customarily and specifically engaged in trade between the Tibet Region of China and India, their wives and children, who are dependent on them for livelihood and their attendants will be allowed entry for purposes of trade into India or the Tibet Region of China, as the case may be, in accordance with custom on the production of certificates duly issued by the local Government of their own country or by its duly authorized agents and examined by the border check-posts of the other party.

(2) Inhabitants of the border districts of the two countries, who cross borders to carry on petty trade or to visit friends and relatives, may proceed to the border districts of the other party as they have

customarily done heretofore and need not be restricted to the passes and route specified in Article IV above and shall not be required to hold passports, visas or permits.

(3) Porters and mule-team drivers of the two countries who cross border to perform necessary transportation services need not hold passports issued by their own country, but shall only hold certificates good for a definite period of time (good for three months, half a year or one year) duly issued by the local Government of their own country or by its duly authorized agents and produce them for registration at the border check-post of the other party.

(4) Pilgrims of both countries need not carry documents of certification but shall register at the border check-post of the other party and shall receive a permit for pilgrimage.

(5) Notwithstanding the provisions of the foregoing paragraph of this article, either Government may refuse entry to any particular person.

(6) Persons who enter the territory of the other party in accordance with the foregoing paragraphs of this article may stay within its territory only after complying with the procedures specified by the other party.

ARTICLE VI

The present agreement shall come into effect upon ratification by both Governments and shall remain in force for eight years. Extension of the present agreement may be negotiated by the two parties if either party requested for it six months prior to the expiry of the agreement and the request is agreed to by the other party.

DONE in duplicate in Peking on the 29th day of April 1954 in the Chinese, Hindi and English languages, all texts being equally valid.

CHANG HAN-FU
Plenipotentiary of the Central People's Government of the People's Republic of China

N. RAGHAVAN
Plenipotentiary of the Government of the Republic of India

(At the same time, there was an exchange of notes between Ambassador Raghavan and Vice-Foreign Minister Chang)

Agreement to Maintain Friendly Relations between the People's Republic of China and the Kingdom of Nepal and on Trade and Intercourse between the Tibet Region of China and Nepal, 1956

The Government of the People's Republic of China and the Government of the Kingdom of Nepal,

Being desirous of further developing the friendly relations between the two countries as good neighbours on the basis of the long-standing friendship between the two peoples,

Reaffirm that the five principles (*Panch Shila*) of:

(1) Mutual respect for each other's territorial integrity and sovereignty,

(2) Non-aggression,

(3) Non-interference in each other's internal affairs for any reasons of an economic, political or ideological character,

(4) Equality and mutual benefit, and

(5) Peaceful co-existence,

Should be the fundamental principles guiding the relations between the two countries.

The two Parties have resolved to conclude the present agreement in accordance with the above-mentioned principles and have for this purpose appointed as their respective plenipotentiaries:

The Government of the People's Republic of China, His Excellency Pan Tzu-li, Ambassador Extraordinary and Plenipotentiary of the People's Republic of China to the Kingdom of Nepal; the Government of the Kingdom of Nepal, His Excellency Chuda Prasad Sharma, Minister for Foreign Affairs of the Kingdom of Nepal, who, having examined each other's credentials and finding them in good and due form, have agreed upon the following:

ARTICLE I

The High Contracting Parties declare that peace and friendship shall be maintained between the People's Republic of China and the Kingdom of Nepal.

ARTICLE II

The High Contracting Parties hereby reaffirm their decision to mutually exchange diplomatic representatives on ambassadorial level.

ARTICLE III

All treaties and documents which existed in the past between China and Nepal including those between the Tibet Region of China and Nepal are hereby abrogated.

ARTICLE IV

In order to maintain and develop the traditional contacts between the peoples of the Tibet Region of China and Nepal the High Contracting Parties agree that the nationals of both Parties may trade, travel and make pilgrimage in those places in each other's territory as agreed upon by both Parties, and the two Parties agree to safeguard the proper interests of the nationals of the other Party in its territory in accordance with the laws of the country of residence, and for this purpose the High Contracting Parties agree to do as follows:

Paragraph I. The High Contracting Parties mutually agree to establish Trade Agencies:

(1) The Chinese Government agrees that the Government of Nepal may establish Trade Agencies at Shigatse, Kyerong and Nyalam;

(2) The Government of Nepal agrees that the Chinese Government may establish an equal number of Trade Agencies in Nepal, the specific locations of which will be discussed and determined at a later date by both Parties;

(3) The Trade Agencies of both Parties shall be accorded the same status and same treatment. The Trade Agents of both Parties shall enjoy freedom from arrest while exercising their functions, and shall enjoy in respect of themselves, their wives and their children who are dependent on them for livelihood freedom from search. The Trade Agencies of both Parties shall enjoy the privileges and immunities for couriers, mailbags and communications in code.

Paragraph II. The High Contracting Parties agree that traders of both countries may trade at the following places:

(1) The Chinese Government agrees to specify (1) Lhasa, (2) Shigatse, (3) Gyantse, and (4) Yatung as markets for trade;

(2) The Government of Nepal agrees that when with the deve-

lopment of Chinese trade in Nepal, it has become necessary to specify markets for trade in Nepal, the Government of Nepal will specify an equal number of markets for trade in Nepal;

(3) Traders of both countries known to be customarily and specifically engaged in border trade between the Tibet Region of China and Nepal may continue trade at the traditional markets for such trade.

Paragraph III. The High Contracting Parties agree that pilgrimage by religious believers of either country to the other may continue according to religious custom. Personal baggages and articles used for pilgrimage carried by the pilgrims of either Party shall be exempted from taxation by the other Party.

Paragraph IV. For travelling across the border between the Tibet Region of China and Nepal, the High Contracting Parties agree that the nationals of both countries shall use the customary routes.

Paragraph V. For travelling across the border by the nationals of the two countries, the High Contracting Parties agree to adopt the following provisions:

(1) Diplomatic personnel and officials of the two countries and nationals of the two countries except those provided by Sub-paragraphs 2, 3 and 4, who travel across the border between the Tibet Region of China and Nepal, shall hold passports issued by their respective countries and visaed by the other Party. Nationals of the two countries who enter the Tibet Region of China or Nepal through a third country shall also hold passports issued by their respective countries and visaed by the other Party.

(2) Traders of the two countries known to be customarily and specifically engaged in trade between the Tibet Region of China and Nepal, their wives and children dependent on them for livelihood and their attendants, not covered by Sub-paragraph 3 of this Paragraph, who enter into the Tibet Region of China or Nepal as the case may be for the purposes of trade, shall hold passports issued by their respective countries and visaed by the other Party, or certificates issued by their respective Governments or by organs authorized by their respective Governments.

(3) Inhabitants of the border districts of the two countries who cross the border to carry on petty trade, to visit friends or relatives, or for seasonal changes of residence, may do so as they have

customarily done heretofore and need not hold passports, visas or other documents of certification.

(4) Pilgrims of either Party who travel across the border between the Tibet Region of China and Nepal for the purposes of pilgrimage need not hold passports, visas or other documents of certifications but shall register at the border check-posts or the first authorized government office of the other Party, and obtain permits for pilgrimage therefrom.

(5) Notwithstanding the provisions of the foregoing Sub-paragraphs of this Paragraph, either Government may refuse entry to any particular person.

(6) Nationals of either country who enter the territory of the other Party in accordance with the foregoing Sub-paragraphs of this Paragraph may stay within the territory only after complying with the procedures specified by the other Party.

ARTICLE V

This Agreement shall be ratified. It shall come into effect after mutual notice of ratifications, and remain in force for eight (8) years. Extension of the present Agreement may be negotiated by the two Parties if either Party requests for it six (6) months prior to the expiry of the Agreement and the request is agreed to by the other Party.

Done in Kathmandu on the 20th day of September 1956, in duplicate in the Chinese, Nepalese and English languages, all texts being equally authentic.

PAN TZU-LI
Plenipotentiary of the Government of the People's Republic of China

CHUDA PRASAD SHARMA
Plenipotentiary of the Government of the Kingdom of Nepal

(At the same time, there was an exchange of notes between Chinese Ambassador Pan Tzu-li and C.P. Sharma, Nepalese Foreign Minister)

Agreement between the Government of the People's Republic of China and the Government of the Union of Burma on the Question of the Boundary between the Two Countries, 1960

The Government of the People's Republic of China and the Government of the Union of Burma,

With a view to promoting an over-all settlement of the Sino-Burmese boundary question and to consolidating and further developing friendly relations between China and Burma,

Have agreed to conclude the present Agreement under the guidance of the Five Principles of Peaceful Co-existence and have agreed as follows:

ARTICLE I

The Contracting Parties agree to set up immediately a joint committee composed of an equal number of delegates from each side and charge it, in accordance with the provisions of the present Agreement, to discuss and work out solutions on the concrete questions regarding the Sino-Burmese boundary enumerated in Article II of the present Agreement, conduct surveys of the boundary and set up boundary markers, and draft a Sino-Burmese boundary treaty. The joint committee shall hold regular meetings in the capitals of the two countries or at any other places in the two countries.

ARTICLE II

The Contracting Parties agree that the existing issues concerning the Sino-Burmese boundary shall be settled in accordance with the following provisions:

(1) With the exception of the area of Hpimaw, Gawlum and Kangfang, the entire undelimited boundary from the High Conical Peak to the western extremity of the Sino-Burmese boundary shall be delimited along the traditional customary line, that is to say, from the High Conical Peak northward along the watershed between the Taiping the Shweli, the Nu (Salween) and the Tulung (Taron) Rivers on the one hand and the Namai Hka River on the other, up to the place where it crosses the Tulung (Taron) River between Chingdam and Nhkumkang, and then along the watershed between the Tulung (Taron) and the Tsayul (Zayul) Rivers on the one hand and all the upper

tributaries of the Irrawaddy River, except for the Tulung (Taron) River, on the other, up to the western extremity of the Sino-Burmese boundary. The joint committee shall send out joint survey teams composed of an equal number of persons from each side to conduct surveys along the above-mentioned watersheds so as to determine the specific alignment of this section of the boundary line and to set up boundary markers.

(2) The Burmese Government has agreed to return to China the area of Hpimaw, Gawlum and Kangfang which belongs to China. As to the extent of this area to be returned to China, it is to be discussed and determined by the joint committee in accordance with the proposals put forward and marked on maps by the Governments of Burma and China on February 4, 1957 and July 26, 1957 respectively. After determining the extent of this area to be returned to China, the joint committee shall send out joint survey teams composed of an equal number of persons from each side to conduct on-the-spot survey of the specific alignment of this section of the boundary line and to set up boundary markers.

(3) In order to abrogate the "perpetual lease" by Burma of the Meng-Mao triangular area (Namwan Assigned Tract) at the junction of the Namwan and the Shweli Rivers, which belongs to China, the Chinese Government has agreed to turn over this area to Burma to become part of the territory of the Union of Burma. In exchange, the Burmese Government has agreed to turn over to China to become part of Chinese territory the areas under the jurisdiction of the Panhung and Panlao tribes, which are west of the boundary line from the junction of the Nam Ting and the Nampa Rivers to the No. 1 marker on the southern delimited section of the boundary as defined in the notes exchanged between the Chinese and the British Governments on June 18, 1941. As to the extent of these areas to be turned over to China, the Chinese and the Burmese Governments put forward proposals marked on maps on July 26, 1957 and June 4, 1959 respectively. The area where the proposals of the two Governments coincide will definitely be turned over to China. Where the proposals of the two Governments differ as to the area under the jurisdiction of the Panhung tribe, the joint committee will send out a team composed of an equal number of persons from each side to ascertain on the spot as to whether it is under the jurisdiction of the Panhung tribe, so as to determine whether it is to be turned over to China. After the extent of the areas under the jurisdiction of the

Panhung and Panlao tribes to be turned over to China has been thus determined, the joint committee will send out joint survey teams composed of an equal number of persons from each side to conduct on-the-spot survey of the specific alignment of this section of the boundary line and to set up boundary markers.

(4) Except for the adjustment provided for in Paragraph (3) of this Article, the section of the boundary from the junction of the Nam Ting and the Nampa Rivers to the No. 1 marker on the southern delimited section of the boundary shall be delimited as defined in the notes exchanged between the Chinese and the British Governments on June 18, 1941. The joint committee shall send out joint survey teams composed of an equal number of persons from each side to carry out delimitation and demarcation along this section of the boundary line and set up boundary markers.

ARTICLE III

The Contracting Parties agree that the joint committee after working out solutions for the existing issues concerning the Sino-Burmese boundary as enumerated in Article II of the present Agreement, shall be responsible for drafting a Sino-Burmese boundary treaty, which shall cover not only all the sections of the boundary as mentioned in Article II of the present Agreement, but also the sections of the boundary which were already delimited in the past and need no adjustment. After being signed by the Governments of the two countries and coming into effect, the new boundary treaty shall replace all old treaties and notes exchanged concerning the boundary between the two countries. The Chinese Government, in line with its policy of being consistently opposed to foreign prerogatives and respecting the sovereignty of other countries, renounces China's right of participation in mining enterprises at Lufang of Burma as provided in the notes exchanged between the Chinese and the British Governments on June 18, 1941.

ARTICLE IV

(1) The present Agreement is subject to ratification and the instruments of ratification will be exchanged in Rangoon as soon as possible.

(2) The present Agreement will come into force immediately on the exchange of the instruments of ratification and shall automatically cease to be in force when the Sino-Burmese boundary treaty to be signed by the two Governments comes into force.

Done in duplicate in Peking on the twenty-eighth day of January 1960, in the Chinese and English languages, both texts being equally authentic.

CHOU EN-LAI
For the Government of the People's Republic of China

NE WIN
For the Government of the Union of Burma

Agreement between the Government of the People's Republic of China and His Majesty's Government of Nepal on the Question of the Boundary between the Two Countries, 1960

The Government of the People's Republic of China and His Majesty's Government of Nepal have noted with satisfaction that the two countries have always respected the existing traditional customary boundary line and lived in amity. With a view to bringing about the formal settlement of some existing discrepancies in the boundary line between the two countries and the scientific delineation and formal demarcation of the whole boundary line, and to consolidating and further developing friendly relations between the two countries, the two Governments have decided to conclude the present Agreement under the guidance of the Five Principles of Peaceful Co-existence and have agreed upon the following:

ARTICLE I

The Contracting Parties have agreed that the entire boundary between the two countries shall be scientifically delineated and formally demarcated through friendly consultations, on the basis of the existing traditional customary line.

ARTICLE II

In order to determine the specific alignment of the boundary line and to enable the fixing of the boundary between the two countries in legal form, the Contracting Parties have decided to set up a joint committee composed of an equal number of delegates from each side and enjoin the committee, in accordance with the provisions of Article III of the present Agreement, to discuss and solve the concrete problems concerning the Sino-Nepalese boundary, conduct survey of the boundary, erect boundary markers, and draft a Sino-Nepalese boundary treaty.   The joint committee will hold its meetings in the capitals or other places of China and Nepal.

ARTICLE III

Having studied the delineation of the boundary line between the two countries as shown on the maps mutually exchanged and the information furnished by each side about its actual jurisdiction over the area bordering on the other country, the Contracting Parties deem that, except for discrepancies in certain sections, their understanding of the traditional customary line is basically the same.   The Contracting Parties have decided to determine concretely the boundary between the two countries in the following ways in accordance with three different cases:

(1)   Sections where the delineation of the boundary line between the two countries on the maps of the two sides is identical,

In these sections the boundary line shall be fixed according to the identical delineation on the maps of the two sides.   The joint committee will send out joint survey teams composed of an equal number of persons from each side to conduct survey on the spot and erect boundary markers.

After the boundary line in these sections is fixed in accordance with the provisions of the above paragraph, the territory north of the line will conclusively belong to China, while the territory south of the line will conclusively belong to Nepal, and neither Contracting Party will any longer lay claim to certain areas within the territory of the other Party.

(2)   Sections where the delineation of the boundary line between the two countries on the maps of the two sides is not identical, whereas the state of actual jurisdiction by each side is undisputed,

The joint committee will send out joint survey teams composed of an equal number of persons from each side to conduct survey on the spot, determine the boundary line and erect boundary markers in these sections in accordance with concrete terrain features (watersheds, valleys, passes, etc.) and the actual jurisdiction by each side.

(3)   Sections where the delineation of the boundary line between the two countries on the maps of the two sides is not identical and the two sides differ in their understanding of the state of actual jurisdiction,

The joint committee will send out joint teams composed of an equal number of persons from each side to ascertain on the spot the state of actual jurisdiction in these sections, make adjustments in accordance with the principles of equality, mutual benefit, friendship and mutual accommodation, determine the boundary line and erect boundary markers in these sections.

ARTICLE IV

The Contracting Parties have decided that, in order to ensure tranquillity and friendliness on the border, each side will no longer dispatch armed personnel to patrol the area on its side within twenty kilometres of the border, but only maintain its administrative personnel and civil police there.

ARTICLE V

The present Agreement is subject to ratification and the instruments of ratification shall be exchanged in Kathmandu as soon as possible.

The present Agreement will come into force immediately on the exchange of the instruments of ratification and will automatically cease to be in force when the Sino-Nepalese boundary treaty to be signed by the two Governments comes into force.

Done in duplicate in Peking on the twenty-first day of March 1960, in the Chinese, Nepalese and English languages, all texts being equally authentic.

CHOU EN-LAI
Plenipotentiary of the Government of the People's Republic of China

B.P. KOIRALA
Plenipotentiary of His Majesty's Government of Nepal

Treaty of Friendship and Mutual Non-Aggression between China and Afghanistan, 1960

The Chairman of the People's Republic of China and His Majesty the King of Afghanistan,

Desiring to maintain and further develop lasting peace and profound friendship between the People's Republic of China and the Kingdom of Afghanistan,

Convinced that the strengthening of good-neighbourly relations and friendly cooperation between the People's Republic of China and the Kingdom of Afghanistan conforms to the fundamental interests of the peoples of the two countries and is in the interest of consolidating peace in Asia and the world,

Have decided for this purpose to conclude the present Treaty in accordance with the fundamental principles of the United Nations Charter and the spirit of the Bandung Conference, and have appointed as their respective Plenipotentiaries:

The Chairman of the People's Republic of China:
Vice-Premier of the State Council and Minister of Foreign Affairs Chen Yi,
His Majesty the King of Afghanistan:
Deputy Prime Minister and Minister of Foreign Affairs Sardar Mohammed Naim.

The above-mentioned Plenipotentiaries, having examined each other's credentials and found them in good and due form, have agreed upon the following:

ARTICLE I

The Contracting Parties recognize and respect each other's independence, sovereignty and territorial integrity.

ARTICLE II

The Contracting Parties will maintain and develop peaceful and friendly relations between the two countries. They undertake to settle all disputes between them by means of peaceful negotiation without resorting to force.

ARTICLE III

Each Contracting Party undertakes not to commit aggression

against the other and not to take part in any military alliance directed against it.

ARTICLE IV

The Contracting Parties have agreed to develop and further strengthen the economic and cultural relations between the two countries in a spirit of friendship and cooperation and in accordance with the principles of equality and mutual benefit and of non-interference in each other's internal affairs.

ARTICLE V

The present Treaty is subject to ratification and the instruments of ratification will be exchanged in Peking as soon as possible.

The present Treaty will come into force immediately on the exchange of the instruments of ratification and will remain in force for a period of ten years.

Unless either of the Contracting Parties gives to the other notice in writing to terminate it at least one year before the expiration of this period, it will remain in force indefinitely, subject to the right of either Party to terminate it after it has been valid for ten years by giving to the other in writing notice of its intention to do so one year before its termination.

Done in duplicate in Kabul on the twenty-sixth day of August 1960, in the Chinese, Persian and English languages, all texts being equally authentic.

CHEN YI
Plenipotentiary of the People's Republic of China

SARDAR MOHAMMED NAIM
Plenipotentiary of the Kingdom of Afghanistan

Appendix II

An Agreement with Persia on the Utilization of Frontier Rivers and Waters from Heri Rud to the Caspian Sea (Extracts), 1926

The Government of the USSR and the Government of Persia, recognizing the need, under Article 3 of the peace treaty between the RSFSR and Persia of 26 February 1921, to determine definite shares in and establish the manner of utilizing frontier rivers and waters from the Heri Rud river to the Caspian Sea, have agreed to conclude the present agreement on this subject, for which purpose they have appointed a mixed commission composed of the following plenipotentiaries: For the Government of the USSR, Alexander Fedorovich Mor and Ivan Ernestovich German; for the Government of Persia, Mirza Seyid Ahmed Khan Moazzami, Hamid Khan Saiyakh, and Mirza Mohammed Khan Maasumkhani.

The said plenipotentiaries, having presented their credentials, which were found to be drawn up in due form and in the customary manner, have agreed to the following:

(1) The waters of the Heri Rud (Tejen) river, beginning from the Pul-i-Khatun bridge, downstream along the entire stretch of the frontier between the contracting parties, shall be divided into ten equal parts, of which three parts shall be for Persian use, and seven parts for the use of the USSR.

The water of the Heri Rud (Tejen) river shall be measured by experts of the contracting parties at the village of Doulet-Abad and on all the canals fed by the Heri Rud (Tejen) river both in Persia and in the USSR along the stretch from the village of Doulet-Abad to the Pul-i-Khatun bridge. The entire quantity of water arrived at as the result of the said measuring shall also be divided into ten equal parts.

In order to ensure a correct division of the water of the Heri Rud (Tejen) river at Doulet-Abad the experts of the contracting parties shall construct a permanent sluice at this place. The costs of construction shall be borne by the contracting parties, who shall mutually approve the construction plans, in proportion to the share of water received by each at this place.

(2) Until the construction of a reservoir (in conformity with Article 3 of the present agreement) the village of Giarmab on Persian territory (15 versts above Pul-i-Khatun) and the Pul-i-Khatun post on the territory of the USSR, shall each have the right of drawing water from the Heri Rud at the rate of 50 litres per second. Should either of the contracting parties take for its village more than 50 litres of water, the surplus shall be counted as part of its share below the Pul-i-Khatun bridge.

(3) Since the distribution of the water of the Heri Rud (Tejen) river determined by the present agreement will not satisfy the require-ments of either of the contracting parties because of the enormous loss of water by the Heri Rud (Tejen) in the spring floods, the two parties recognize the expediency of constructing a reservoir on the Heri Rud above Pul-i-Khatun to hold the surplus water for the use of the contracting parties.

The contracting parties agree to the construction of such a reservoir to the necessary technical survey of the locality, and to the conclusion of a special agreement on the construction and exploitation of the reservior and the terms for the division of its waters.

(4) All the water of the Chaacha river and of all its tributaries shall be divided into two equal parts, of which one shall be for the use of Persia and the other shall be allowed to pass on to the territory of the USSR.

The water of the Chaacha river shall be measured by the experts of the contracting parties at the frontier and on all the canals fed by the Chaacha on Persian territory, from the frontier to the point of confluence of the Abegiarm and Khour rivers (at the village of Amir-Abad). The total quantity of water arrived at by the said measuring shall be divided into two equal parts.

(Under Articles 5, 6, 7, 8, 14, 15, and 16 similar provisions to those in Article 4 are made relating to the rivers Meana, Kelat Chai, Archinian, Lain-su-Chandyr, Sumbar, and Atrek.)

(9) All the water of the Kazgan Chai (Zenginanlu river) shall be divided into five equal parts, of which two parts shall be for the use of Persia and three for the use of the USSR.

The water of the Kazgan Chai (Zenginanlu river) shall be measured by the experts of the contracting parties at the frontier and on all the canals fed by the Kazgan Chai (Zenginanlu river) on Persian territory from the frontier up to and including the place above the village of Zenginanlu where the village draws its water. The total quantity of water arrived at by the said measuring shall be divided into five parts, of which the Persian share (2/5) shall include that amount of water which flows through Soviet territory from Kazgan Chai to supply the Liutfabad district.

The Government of the USSR undertakes to allow the unhindered passage by the canal passing through its territory of that quantity of water which Persia allocates from its share for the use of the Liutfabad district.

In order to supply water to the Liutfabad district the Persian Government is granted by the Government of the USSR the right to conduct the water by the old Babajik canal instead of through the present canal or to build a new canal on the territory of the USSR. The USSR grants Persia this right free of charge.

The place where the new canal is to be built shall be determined by agreement with the Government of the USSR.

All expenditure incurred in the restoration of the Babajik canal or the construction of a new canal shall be borne by the Persian Government.

The Government of the USSR undertakes to allow unhindered passage on to its territory of Persian nationals, furnished with the requisite papers, appointed to clean and repair the canal serving the Liutfabad district.

(10) The Persian Government undertakes to release to the USSR from the Giulriz river into the canal on Soviet territory 10 litres of water per second (1/2 senga) for the use of the Artyk station.

To measure this water the USSR shall build at the frontier on its territory and at its expense and in the presence of an expert from the Persian side a new sluice.

(11)   All the water of the Durungiar river and of the salt springs in the river Durungiar valley shall be entirely for the use of Persia.

(12)   All the water of the Kelte Chinar river shall be for the use of Persia.

The Persian Government undertakes not to hamper nationals of the USSR in using the waters of the springs on Persian territory in the valley of the Kelte Chinar river (below the Persian village of Kelte Chinar) which nationals of the USSR are using at the present time, and also to allow unhindered passage to Soviet nationals furnished with the requisite papers to clean and to work on these springs and on the bed of the river which they supply.

(13)   All the water of the river Firiuzinka (Firiuza) shall, after the needs of the village of Firiuza have been met, be for the use of the Soviet villages downstream . . . .

(15)   Should the USSR, after the signature of the present agreement, erect on its territory by the river Sumbar hydrotechnical installations to retain water, the Government of the USSR undertakes to allow as much water to flow into the Atrek river in the irrigation period as would have passed in the absence of these installations in the given meteorological conditions.   The USSR shall inform Persia in advance of its intention to erect such installations.

(16)   Should Persia after the signature of the present agreement erect by the river Atrek on its territory hydrotechnical installations to retain water, the Persian Government undertakes to allow in the irrigation period as much water to pass to the frontier between Persia and the USSR where the division of the Atrek river water begins as would have passed in the absence of such installations in the given meteorological conditions.   Persia shall inform the USSR in advance of its intention to erect such installations.

(17)   The waters mentioned in the present agreement shall be measured at the request of Persia or the USSR by the experts and water officers of the contracting parties jointly and for each separate river and the canals fed by it simultaneously.

Persia and the USSR mutually undertake to allow unhampered access on to their territory of the experts and water officers authorized to execute the works on the rivers mentioned in the present agreement if furnished with the requisite documents, which shall indicate the place for crossing the frontier.

(18)   The waters on the frontier shall be measured at the most convenient places within 200 metres of the frontier on the Persian or

Soviet side. The places shall be selected by mutual agreement between the experts of the contracting parties.

At the places selected for measurement the Soviet experts shall erect, at the cost of the USSR and in the presence of an expert from the Persian side, a hydrometric post for each river, consisting of three water gauge racks, one levelling mark, and one light service bridge; the river bed shall if necessary be put in proper order.

The experts and water officers of the USSR and of Persia shall have equal rights to use the hydrometric posts.

(19)   Should differences arise between the water officers of the contracting parties on any question of water utilization, these questions shall be submitted for joint settlement to the following representatives of Persia and the USSR (who may be represented by their deputies): for the Heri Rud (Tejen) river, the Governor of Serakh for Persia, and the Serakh district water officers for the USSR; for the Chaacha, Meana (Kara Tikan), and Kelat Chai (Nafte) rivers, the Governor of Kelat for Persia and the Dushak district water officer for the USSR....

(20)   If the provisions of the present agreement in regard to the sharing of the waters of the frontier rivers and waters and their mutual utilization be violated by the nationals of the contracting parties, both parties are obliged to take immediately on their own territory the necessary steps to rectify the infringement, to conduct an investigation, and to make the guilty parties responsible under law for their acts.

(21)   The sharing and method of utilization of the frontier waters laid down in the present agreement shall be brought by the contracting parties to the attention of their local frontier authorities and of the populations of the districts adjacent to the rivers within one month of the signature of the agreement.

(22)   The present agreement is subject to ratification within six months of its signature.   Ratifications shall be exchanged in Teheran.

(23)   The present agreement enters into force immediately on its signature.

(24)   The present agreement, consisting of twenty-four articles, is drawn up in the Russian and Persian languages in two authentic copies.   Both texts shall be considered authentic.

Done in Poltoratsky (Askhabad) 20 February 1926 (I Esfand 1304).

Convention with Turkey for the Regulation of the Use of Frontier Waters, and Protocol, 1927

The Central Executive Committee of the USSR on the one part, and the Turkish Republic on the other, animated by the desire that cordial relations and sincere friendship, based on mutual interests, may reign for ever between them, have decided in the interests of both parties to conclude a convention on the use of the waters of frontier rivers, streams, and brooks, and for this purpose have appointed as their plenipotentiaries:

> for the USSR: O. Karklin, A. Kalandadze, S. Shadunts;
> for the Turkish Republic: Fahri Bey, Vehbi Bey, Hassan Bey, Jemal Bey;

who, having exchanged their full powers, which were found to be in due and proper form, have agreed to the following provisions:

(1)   The two contracting parties shall each use half of the water of the rivers, streams, and brooks which coincide with the line of the frontier between the USSR and the Turkish Republic.

(2)   Each contracting party reserves the right to retain all the installations for water utilization which are in existence at the moment the present convention is signed.   They may be repaired and their structure restored and shall be maintained and repaired by the contracting party to which they belong in accordance with the technical requirements of water utilization.

(3)   In order to divide the water and to study the flow of the rivers, the two contracting parties shall set up hydrometric observation posts (posts for determining cross sections, flood marks, and rates of flow).

Both parties shall have the right to determine the cross sections of the river bed along those stretches of the rivers where the quantity of water is to be ascertained.

The places for the hydrometric observation posts shall be selected by a mixed commission composed of an equal number of representatives of the two contracting parties.

(4)   To determine the flow of the river waters the two contracting parties shall establish a mixed commission on a parity basis which twice a year, from 15 June to 1 July and from 1 September to 15 September, shall determine at the hydrometric observation posts the flow

of water in the rivers falling within the present convention and shall jointly draw up a report on the quantity of water.

The mixed commission shall be formed of two representatives of each of the contracting parties.

If one of the contracting parties, should the level of water in the rivers fall, declares it to be necessary to determine the flow of water at the appropriate hydrometric observation posts at other times than those set forth above, the other party is obliged to send its representatives within fifteen days from the day when the declaration was made to the respective Government of the wish to take measurements. If the representatives of one of the parties do not arrive within the stated time, the other party has the right to determine by itself the flow of water in the rivers but the results of the determination of the flow must be communicated to the other party.

Should the other party itself measure the same flow and arrive at different results, it has the right to demand that new measurements be taken.

The two contracting parties shall share equally the joint costs of the determination by the mixed commission of the flow of water in the rivers.

(5) Should it be necessary to raise the level of water in the rivers and to make artificial reservoirs in order to construct irrigation canals, each of the contracting parties shall have the right to construct barrages.

(a) When a barrage is erected by one of the contracting parties the quantity of water due to the other party must be allowed to pass freely by the barrage or the reservoir, and free passage for fish shall also be ensured.

(b) While the barrage is being erected both contracting parties shall have the right to use both banks of the river for preliminary works and for the provisional passage of water while the work is in progress, and also to erect all kinds of hydrotechnical installations, temporary embankment, defensive works, etc. These installations however shall not divert the water for more than 250 metres from the construction site.

(c) The party constructing the barrage shall take all measures to protect the interest of the other contracting party from any injury which might result from its work, and when the work is completed shall compensate the other contracting party for any material damage if such damage occurred despite the measures taken.

A special agreement between the two Governments is required in each case for the erection of barrages which can be used as bridges.

(6) To protect the banks of the rivers which form the frontier from undermining by water, each contracting party retains the right to build buttresses, provided that it protects the other party from any harmful consequences from such building.

(7) Neither of the contracting parties may artificially change the direction of the river channel. Should the frontier rivers be deflected from their bed, both parties shall have the right to carry out regulating and repair works on both banks of the said rivers, due warning being given to the other contracting party.

(8) Both parties reserve the right to erect hydro-electric stations and mills, but the places for diverting and channelling the water for the said stations and establishments should be close to each other and sited in such a way that no injury is caused to the other party, and that the part of the river (the free part) used by the hydro-electric station or mill does not encroach on original installations already in existence or projected for the construction of irrigation canals and the various other installations of the contracting parties provided for in the present convention.

(9) Each party has the right to install pumps on condition that only that part of the water is used which is due to the interested party.

(10) The final selection of the siting and type of installations referred to in Articles 3, 5, 6, 7, 8, and 9 of the present convention shall be made and laid down by the mixed commission mentioned in the preceding articles.

The date for convening the mixed commission will be fixed not later than three months from the day when its convening is requested by one of the two parties.

The party which takes the initiative in convening the mixed commission shall send the Government of the other party, at the same time as the proposal for its meeting, a sketch plan of the proposed installation.

In the event of differences of opinion in the mixed commission all questions in dispute shall be referred for final settlement to the Governments of the two parties.

(11) Nationals of both contracting parties have the right to use on equal terms the waters forming the frontier between the USSR and the Turkish Republic on the following conditions:

(*i*) Nationals of both contracting parties may use the rivers and streams coinciding with the line of the frontier and used for mills, irrigations, watering, and fishing during the hours of day-light without special permission.

Approach to the river bank at night, if found necessary for essential purposes, is permitted only at points to be mutually agreed upon by the frontier authorities of the two States.

(*ii*) Cattle brought to water shall not cross into the territory of the other party.

Should cattle by accident cross the frontier the herdsman shall be allowed to cross the frontier not farther than 50 metres to lead the cattle back as quickly as possible.

Watering places shall be selected and agreed by the frontier authorities of the two parties.

(*iii*) Each party has the right to fish from its bank. Fishing at night is forbidden.

(*iv*) The present article does not apply to the following rivers and streams: Arax, Arapa Chai, Poskhov Chai, Kura, and Chorokh.

(12) The present convention is subject to ratification within two months of its signature.

It will enter into force upon the exchange of ratifications. The instruments of ratification shall be exchanged as soon as possible at Ankara.

The present convention shall remain in force for five years. Should neither of the contracting parties take steps to denounce or amend the convention by the end of that time, it shall remain in force for another year and shall be valid so long as no steps are taken to denounce or amend it.

In witness whereof the aforesaid plenipotentiaries have signed the present convention and affixed thereto their seals.

Done in two copies in French at Kars, 8 January 1927.

PROTOCOL

The undersigned (here follow the names given in the convention) have agreed as follows:

(1) In conformity with article 5 of the convention signed at Kars, 8 January 1927 on the use of the waters of frontier rivers, streams, and brooks between the USSR and the Turkish Republic, the Government of the Turkish Republic grants the Government of the USSR

the right to build on the River Arax, at an approximate distance of 750 metres upstream from the Karakale bridge, a barrage for the Sardarabad Canal being constructed by the USSR; for this purpose the Government of the USSR is authorized to engage in the essential survey work on the Turkish bank of the River Arax, and to undertake works for the construction of the barrage.

The barrage is to be of the type shown in the sketch plan attached to the present protocol.

(2)   The area in which the survey work is to be done, and the superficial area required for building the barrage on the Turkish bank of the Arax, are fixed by the following measurements:

(*i*)   for survey work an area in length equal to 1,400 metres upstream from the Karakale bridge, and in width equal to 80 metres.

(*ii*)   for constructing the dam an area equal in length to 800 metres starting from the same point, and in width 150 metres.

(3)   The Government of the USSR grants the Government of the Turkish Republic the right to take the waters of the aforesaid reservoir by means of a canal to be subsequently built by Turkey to irrigate the fields of the Ighdir Valley, to the extent of 50 per cent of the water therein and on the following conditions:

(*i*)   The Turkish Republic undertakes to share in the cost of construction of the Sardarabad a barrage in proportion to the amount of water used and to the economic benefits which the barrage confers on the two parties;

(*ii*)   The Turkish Republic reserves the right to make use when it so wishes of this barrage provided it pays the cost provided for in Paragraph (*i*) of this article. The time of payment for the costs in question shall be agreed between the Governments of the two contracting parties.

(4)   In order to prevent the canals of the Ighdir Valley from drying up, the Government of the USSR, which is constructing the Sardarabad barrage, undertakes to ensure that, until the Turkish Republic shall enjoy the use of the Sardarabad reservoir by taking water from it by means of a canal, the said canals take the same amount of water that they took before the construction of the aforesaid barrage.

In particular, in order that half the water of the river may be directed towards and close by the Turkish bank during the dry season, it also undertakes to build by the Turkish bank a lock similar to that which is to be constructed by the Soviet bank, and to regulate the river bed from the lock to the beginning of the Ighdir Valley canals in such a way that the water cannot extend over the entire bed.

The USSR, which is building the barrage, shall defray the costs of the aforesaid works.

(5) The Government of the USSR, which is building the barrage, shall take all the steps necessary to protect the interests of the Turkish Government from any injury which may be caused by its building and, when the work is completed, shall compensate the Turkish Republic for any material damage if such damage, despite the precautions taken, shall have been caused.

(6) The Turkish Government reserves the right to inspect the building of the barrage, of the type shown in the sketch plan attached to the present protocol.

(7) The present protocol is subject to ratification within two months of its signature.

It enters into force upon the exchange of ratifications.

The instruments of ratification shall be exchanged at Ankara as soon as possible.

In witness whereof the aforesaid delegates have signed the present protocol and attached thereto their seals.

Done in two copies in French at Kars, 8 January 1927.

Soviet-Persian Notes on the Appointment of Frontier Commissioners, 14 August 1927

I

Herewith I have the honour to inform you that with the object of preventing any kind of frontier incident occurring on the Soviet-Persian border, and also with the object of settling quickly such incidents as occur, the Government of the USSR considers it appropriate to make the following arrangements:

agreement on the arrangements noted above for their activities.

II

Herewith I have the honour to confirm the receipt of your postal note of 14 August concerning the consent of the Persian Government to the arrangements proposed in my note of 14 August for frontier commissioners.

In regard to your explanation of the paragraph in my note which runs:

The said commissioners are obliged to see that any kind of event or other happening occurring along the common frontier of the contracting parties which threatens to disturb order along the frontier or may be the cause of disputes between the frontier inhabitants of the two States, or violate the interests which the two parties have in virtue of valid treaties and agreements, is prevented...

I have the honour to inform you that my Government agrees with the explanation given in your note, that:

The frontier commissioners must prevent any kind of aggressive action by bandits or frontier inhabitants against the frontier inhabitants of the other party, and contraband activity, and shall see to the maintenance of order on the frontier, and in no case shall the commissioners of either party have the right to intervene in questions relating to the determination of the frontier, or in political and other internal affairs of the other State.

At the same time I have the honour to inform you that the names of the Soviet frontier commissioners will be submitted to you in the next few days, and I hope that the Persian Government for its part will be so good as to present its commissioners, who are to be sent to the Soviet-Persian frontier.

In conclusion may I express my conviction, which I hope that you, Mr Minister, share, that the appointment of the frontier commissioners will help to promote the peaceful productive labour of the frontier inhabitants and the further consolidation of the profoundly friendly relations existing between the peoples and Governments of the USSR and Persia.

Convention with Turkey on the Investigation and Settlement of Frontier Disputes, 1928

In order to simplify the investigation and settlement of minor frontier disputes and incidents

The Government of the USSR on the one hand, and the Government of the Turkish Republic on the other, have decided to conclude a convention, and have therefore authorized:

> The Government of the USSR:
> Yakov Surits, plenipotentiary representative of the USSR,
> Vladimir Potemkin, Counsellor to the Embassy of the USSR,
> Andrei Ivanchenko,
> Andrei Kalandadze.
> The Government of the Turkish Republic:
> His Excellency Zekiai Bey, deputy for Diarbekir.

The said delegates, having presented their credentials, which were found to be adequate and drawn up in the appropriate manner, have agreed as follows:

(1) All minor frontier incidents and disputes (Article 2) which may arise after the entry into force of the present convention, shall be decided on the spot by the bodies and in the manner set forth in articles 3-14 of this convention.

Note: All frontier incidents and disputes which occurred before the entry into force of this convention shall be settled by diplomatic means. With the mutual consent of the People's Commissariat for Foreign Affairs of the USSR and the Ministry for Foreign Affairs of the Turkish Republic, these matters may be examined and settled in the manner set forth in the present convention for minor incidents and disputes.

(2) The term minor frontier incidents and disputes in the present convention is understood to mean:

(*a*) isolated cases of shooting at posts, sentries, and private persons in the frontier area, provided that such shooting does not cause death, wounding, or material damage;

(*b*) crossing of the frontier without the necesssary permission by local residents, customs officials, or frontier guards, provided that such crossing is of an accidental character and not affected with evil intent;

(*c*) detention of domestic animals which have crossed the frontier;

(*d*) carrying off cattle or other property from across the frontier;

(*e*) the crossing of the frontier by armed persons, provided it is not of a political character;

(*f*) damage to installations on water or land which are in the direct neighbourhood of the frontier;

(*g*) other frontier incidents and misunderstandings of the same character.

(3) The representatives of the frontier authorities authorized to examine and settle minor frontier incidents and disputes are: for the USSR the frontier commissioner, the same being in command of the frontier area; for the Turkish Republic, the chief frontier officer, or persons authorized by them.

The area of operations of the said functionaries and their permanent station shall be determined in a protocol to be attached to the present convention.

(4) Decisions concerning the matters to be examined by the frontier commissioners or persons authorized by them referred to in Article 3 of the present convention shall be taken by mutual agreement between the said functionaries of the USSR and the Turkish Republic. These decisions are to be put in writing in the briefest possible form, drawn up and signed in two copies, one in the Russian and one in the Turkish language.

(5) Should agreement not be reached, the matter is to be transferred for settlement by the Governments of the contracting parties. In these cases the above-mentioned functionaries of each party shall only undertake an investigation, and each side shall send the material collected to the People's Commissariat for Foreign Affairs of the USSR and the Ministry for Foreign Affairs of the Turkish Republic respectively.

(6) The decisions of the functionaries referred to in Article 3 concerning questions indicated in paragraphs (*a*), (*b*), (*c*), (*e*) and (*g*) of Article 2, and also decisions on the return of detained property and cattle, are binding on both sides.

Should it be impossible to make compensation in kind of stolen property or cattle, and also in regard to losses referred to in paragraph (*f*) of Article 2, the commissioners shall confine themselves to establishing the facts; compensation for the property, cattle, or losses shall be made by the guilty persons in the manner required by the laws of each of the two countries.

(7) The functionaries referred to in Article 3 shall by mutual agreement set up special control and crossing stations, where statements and letters on these matters shall be drawn up, frontier questions examined, and decisions taken put into effect, in particular, the readmission of persons detained by one of the contracting parties, and the return of animals and property.

(8) The frontier commissioners of each party and persons authorized by them have the right to cross the frontier in order to proceed to the meeting places mentioned in Article 10 on business connected with the investigation of frontier incidents and disputes on the basis of documents issued, for the USSR, by the local frontier authorities and the local agents of the People's Commissariat for Foreign Affairs, and for the Turkish Republic, by the chief frontier officer.

These documents shall be endorsed for each separate crossing of the frontier by the functionaries (Article 3) of the other contracting party at the control and crossing stations mentioned in the attached protocol.

(9) To facilitate the settlement of conflicts the functionaries referred to in Article 3 of the present convention have the right, should the need arise, to issue permits to complainants, witnesses, or experts of their country for a one-time crossing of the frontier. These permits shall be endorsed by the functionaries of the other contracting party.

Plaintiffs, witnesses, and experts shall not carry arms on the territory of the other party.

(10) Meetings between the functionaries referred to in Article 3 to investigate and settle frontier incidents and disputes shall take place at the meeting places or frontier crossing stations mentioned in the protocol attached to this convention, on the proposal of either party.

(11) The functionaries referred to in Article 3 shall, when on the territory of the other party for the purpose of settling frontier incidents and disputes, enjoy personal immunity and the right to wear the uniform of their service.

The said persons have the right to transport duty free food supplies

stationed at Aivaj, and the chief of the Sary-Chashmensk frontier section, stationed in the village of Sary-Chashme.

(e) The head of the Kala-i-Khumb frontier section, stationed in the town of Kala-i-Khumb and with an area of operations from the rock on the bank of the Pianj River 42 kilometres north-east of the village of Shoonak to the junction of the rivers Yaz-Gulem and Pianj.

(f) The head of the Khorog frontier section, stationed in the town of Khorog and with an area of operations from the river Yaz-Gulem to the junction of the Soviet-Afghan-Chinese frontier.

His assistants shall be: the chief of the Ishkashim frontier section, stationed at Ishkashim, and the chief of the Liangar frontier section, stationed at Liangar.

(3) The commissioners of each State shall be subjects or citizens of that State. Neither of the contracting States may appoint as commissioners persons who were formerly subjects or citizens of the other State. When appointing the commissioners, each Government shall inform the other about the appointments made. In order that the frontier commissioners may carry out their work in an orderly and uninterrupted fashion, the parties consider it necessary that the procedure for presenting the frontier commissioners to the Government of the other party shall be completed rapidly, by telegraph. The parties shall give instructions to their frontier authorities that frontier commissioners who are being replaced shall not leave their sections before the arrival for duty of those who are to replace them.

(4) The frontier commissioners are bound to prevent in the frontier area any kind of aggressive action by criminals against the frontier residents of the other party and to see to the maintenance of order on the frontier, and they are also bound to take energetic steps to see that in no case shall arms be fired from the territory of one party against the posts, sentries, or private persons or territory of the other party. Should such actions nevertheless by chance take place, they must immediately put a stop to them and make an investigation. In the first place the frontier commissioners must take decisive and energetic steps to liquidate those criminals on their territory in regard to whom commissioners have the right to present to the other party a list of the names of the criminals to be found on the territory of the other party and liable to liquidation or to expulsion from the frontier region into the interior of the country. If there is a likelihood that the pursued

persons may cross into the territory of the other party, the frontier commissioners of the first party is bound to inform the frontier commissioner of the other party in good time so that the necessary steps shall be duly taken to liquidate these criminals on the territory of his State.   Should there be frontier violations or persecutions by the inhabitants of one party of the inhabitants of the other party, the commissioner of the injured party shall report on this to the commissioner from whose area the disturbance of order proceeded, after which the two commissioners jointly shall proceed to the place where the incident occurred to investigate the matter. The commissioner in whose area the preparations were made is bound to take with all possible speed the steps necessary to liquidate the incident.

Note: The frontier area is reckoned as an area extending to a depth of eighteen (18) kilometres.

(5) The category of questions referred to in Article 4, and subject to joint settlement by the frontier commissioners, includes:

(*a*) accidental crossing of the frontier by inhabitants of the frontier area (excluding frontier officials of both parties) and help in returning them to their own territory;

(*b*) shooting from the territory of one party at the posts, sentries, private persons, or the territory of the other party;

(*c*) crossing by armed persons or armed gangs of brigands from the territory of one State on to the territory of the other;

(*d*) accidental crossing of domestic animals and herds (large and small cattle) from the territory of one party to the territory of the other, stealing property and cattle from across the frontier, and also the transporting of raw materials and industrial products and the driving of cattle by contraband means from the territory of one party to the territory of the other;

(*e*) damage to farms, property, and other equipment, including river and irrigation works, in the immediate neighbourhood of the frontier;

(*f*) all other frontier incidents of a local character.

Note: Questions concerning the determination of the frontier, and also questions of a political or economic character, for which no provision has been made in the present note, do not lie within the competence of the frontier commissioners.

(6) Should a frontier incident occur, the commissioner of the party on whose territory it occurs must inform the commissioner of

the other party immediately of what has taken place, after which both commissioners must without any delay proceed together to the scene of the incident to make the necessary investigations and take the necessary steps, and also to draw up and sign a protocol. They may settle frontier incidents by mutual agreement.

(7) Where incidents require that measures shall be taken immediately the commissioner of each party has the right, should the commissioner of the other party be absent from the spot, to turn to the local authorities of the other party, so that the matter may then be brought to the notice of the commissioner of the other party, and in case of need they shall jointly undertake a supplementary investigation and take supplementary measures. The parties shall draw up and sign a protocol on the results of the investigation of the incident, both by the local authorities, and by the supplementary investigation, and on the measures taken in the one and the other case. The list of incidents to be treated as matters of urgency shall be drawn up by agreement of the commissioners of both parties, and until such agreement is reached, the frontier commissioners may not appeal directly to the local authorities of the other party. In cases of the utmost urgency and in the absence of the commissioner of the other party, the frontier commissioners may appeal to the local authorities regardless of whether or not the matter at issue is included among the questions on which the frontier commissioners had previously agreed.

(8) The commissioners' decisions and minutes are to be drawn up in two original copies, in the State language of the two parties, and as briefly as possible.

(9) Should the commissioners not reach agreement on an incident which has occurred, the question is to be immediately transferred for settlement by diplomatic means.

(10) The frontier commissioners of both parties shall enjoy the following rights:

(a) they may cross the frontier at places mutually agreed upon by the commissioners and on the basis of documents giving their official position, and may be accompanied by an interpreter, a secretary, and an assistant. These latter persons may cross the frontier on the production of documents issued to them by their frontier commissioner. All the documents mentioned in the present paragraph shall be stamped by the representatives of the other party with a visa for a fixed period. In addition, persons with such documents are obliged whenever they cross the frontier to present their passports to the frontier authorities of the other party;

(b) the commissioners have the right, in case of need, to give permission to injured parties, witnesses, and experts of their side to cross the frontier once in both directions, but the number of such persons shall not exceed ten (10);

(c) injured parties, experts, and witnesses crossing into the territory of the other party in the said manner, shall not carry arms;

(d) the frontier commissioners of both parties, and also their official correspondence, shall enjoy immunity on the territory of both parties;

(e) the frontier commissioners shall enjoy the right to wear the uniform of their service;

(f) the frontier commissioners are entitled to use codes in their correspondence with the political representatives and consuls of their State;

(g) the frontier commissioners shall enjoy the right of transporting duty free stores of provisions and of all articles required by them for the execution of their duties, such as office equipment. The weight of such luggage shall not exceed fifteen kilograms per person. Such luggage is liable to the usual customs inspection.

(11) Each party shall bear the cost of the upkeep and travelling expenses while on duty of its frontier commissioners, and shall enjoy the co-operation of the other party in regard to getting means of transport and lodging, and also in regard to the granting of documents required in an investigation, and in receiving depositions from such persons as may be required.

(12) Should it be necessary for the frontier commissioner of one of the parties to question a witness or injured party on the territory of the other party, the questioning shall be conducted by the frontier commissioner of the party to which the witness or injured party belongs, in the presence of the frontier commissioner of the other party.

(13) The first meeting of the frontier commissioners to organize the future work in their area shall take place not later than one month after the exchange of notes setting up the frontier commissioner service.

(14) Should a frontier commissioner of one party take any action in regard to the other party exceeding the limits of his competence or in contradiction to his duties, the other party shall have the right to

request his removal and his replacement by another commissioner.

(15) Everything set forth above in regard to the frontier commissioners, including the method of their appointment as provided for in the third article of the present note, shall, in the absence of any commissioner, be extended to his assistant, who shall have the same powers.

(16) Should it be necessary to change the number of sections of the frontier commissioners, to change the area of their operations, their duties and rights, or the place of their residence as given in the second article of the present note, all such changes will be effected by agreement between the plenipotentiary representative of the USSR in Afghanistan and the Ministry for Foreign Affairs of the Kingdom of Afghanistan, or between the People's Commissariat for Foreign Affairs of the USSR and the Embassy of the Kingdom of Afghanistan in Moscow, by means of a supplementary exchange of notes.

(17) The agreement set forth in the present note will remain in force for three (3) years. Thereafter it shall remain in force without a time limit, each side having the right to denounce it by giving notice six (6) months in advance to the other party.

In submitting the above for your consideration, I have the honour to request you to inform me of the opinion of the Afghan Government on this matter.

Should the Government of Afghanistan agree to the above, will you be good enough to inform me of the places of residence and the area of operations of the Afghan frontier commissioners.

(The Afghan reply of the same date is, *mutatis mutandis*, in identical terms.)

Bibliography

Ludwig W. Adamec, *Afghanistan, 1900-1923: A Diplomatic History* (Berkeley/ Los Angeles, 1967).

Edward Allworth, ed., *Central Asia: A Century of Russian Rule* (New York, 1967).

J.F. Baddeley, *Russia, Mongolia, China: Being Some Record of the Relations between them from the Beginning of XVth Century to the Death of Tsar Alexei Nikhailovich A.D. 1602-1672* (London, 1919), 2 vols.

C.R. Bawden, *The Modern History of Mongolia* (London, 1968).

S. Becker, *Russia's Protectorates in Central Asia: Bukhara and Khiva, 1865-1924* (Cambridge, Mass., 1968).

Charles Bell, *Tibet Past and Present* (Oxford, 1924).

L.V.S. Blacker, *On Secret Patrol in High Asia* (London, 1922).

Edmund Candler, *The Unveiling of Lhasa* (London, 1905).

Olaf Caroe, *Wells of Power* (London, 1951).

_____, *The Soviet Empire: The Turks of Central Asia and Stalinism* (London, 1953).

Vincent Chen, *Sino-Russian Relations in the Seventeenth Century* (The Hague, (1966).

Cheng Tien-fong, *A History of Sino-Russian Relations* (Washington, 1957).

O. Edmund Clubb, *China and Russia: The "Great Game"* (New York, 1971).

George N. Curzon, *Russia in Central Asia in 1889 and the Anglo-Russian Question* (London, 1889).

_____, *Persia and the Persian Question* (London, 1892), 2 vols.

C. Collin Davies, *The Problem of the North-West Frontier 1890-1908 with a Survey of Policy since 1849* (Cambridge, 1932).

W.A. Douglas Jackson, *Russo-Chinese Borderlands* (Princeton, N.J., 1962).

Algernon Durand, *The Making of a Frontier* (London, 1900).

C.H. Ellis, *The Transcaspian Episode 1918-1919* (London, 1963).

Peter Fleming, *Bayonets to Lhasa* (London, 1961).

Gerard M. Fritters, *Outer Mongolia and its International Position* (Baltimore, Md., 1949).

R.L. Greaves, *Persia and the Defence of India* (London, 1959).

F.A. Golder, *Russian Expansion on the Pacific, 1641-1850* (Cleveland, Ohio, 1914).

Gavin Hambly, ed., *Central Asia* (London, 1969).

John A. Harrison, *The Founding of the Russian Empire in Asia and America* (Miami, Fla, 1971).

T.H. Holdich, *The Indian Borderland, 1880-1900* (London, 1901).

Charles Warren Hostler, *Turkism and the Soviets* (London, 1957).

Immanual Hsu, *The Ili Crisis (1871-81): A Study of Sino-Russian Diplomacy, 1878-1881* (Oxford, 1965).

Harish Kapur, *Soviet Russia and Asia, 1917-1927: A Study of Soviet Policy Towards Turkey, Iran and Afghanistan* (Geneva, 1965).

Devendra Kaushik, *Central Asia in Modern Times: A History from the Early Nineteenth Century* (Moscow, 1970).

Firuz Kazemzadeh, *The Struggle for Transcaspia, 1917-1921* (Oxford, 1952).

Robert J. Kerner, *The Urge to the Sea: The Course of Russian History* (Berkeley, 1942).

N.A. Khalfin, *Russia's Policy in Central Asia, 1857-68* (London, 1964).

Alastair Lamb, *China-India Border* (London, 1964).

———, *The McMahon Line: A Study in the Relations between India, China and Tibet, 1904-1914* (London, 1966).

George V. Lantzeff, *Siberia in the Seventeenth Century* (Berkeley, 1943).

Owen Lattimore, *Inner Asian Frontiers of China* (New York, 1940).

———, *Nationalism and Revolution in Mongolia* (New York, 1955).

G. Lenczowski, *Russia and the West in Iran* (New York, 1949).

Li Tieh-tseng, *The Historical Status of Tibet* (New York, 1956).

J.A. MacGahan, *Campaigning on the Oxus, and the Fall of Khiva* (New York, 1874).

George McMunn, *Romance of the Indian Frontiers* (London, 1936).

James William Morley, *The Japanese Thrust into Siberia, 1918* (New York, 1957).

George G.S. Murphy, *Soviet Mongolia: A Study of the Oldest Political Satellite* (Berkeley/Los Angeles, 1966).

Guenther Nollan and Hans Juergen Wiehe, *Russia's South Flank* (London, 1964).

Martin R. Norins, *Gateway to Asia: Sinkiang, Frontier of the Chinese Far West* (New York, 1944).

Frederick O'Conner, *On the Frontier and Beyond : A Record of Thirty Years' Service* (London, 1931).

Alexander G. Park, *Bolshevism in Turkestan, 1917-1927* (New York, 1957).

Michel N. Pavlosky, *Chinese-Russian Relations* (New York, 1949).

L. Petech, *China and Tibet in the Early 18th Century: History of the Establishment of Chinese Protectorate in Tibet* (Leiden, 1950).

Richard A Pierce, *Russian Central Asia, 1867-1917: A Study in Colonial Rule* (Berkeley/Los Angeles, 1960).

E.G. Ravenstein, *The Russians on the Amur* (London, 1892).

Ravinder Kumar, *India and the Persian Gulf Region, 1858-1907* (Bombay, 1965).

Robert A. Rupen, *Mongols of the Twentieth Century* (The Hague, 1964), 2 vols.

Nari Rustomji, *Enchanted Frontiers : Bhutan, Sikkim and India's North-Eastern Borderlands* (Bombay, 1971).

Harrison E. Salisbury, *The Coming War between Russia and China* (London, 1969).

Eugene Schuyler, *Turkistan : Notes of Journey in Russian Turkistan, Khokand, Bukhara, and Kuldja* (New York/London, 1877), 2 vols.

W.D. Shakabpa, *Tibet : A Political History* (New Haven, 1967).

Harry Schwartz, *Tsars, Mandarins, and Commissars* (New York, 1964).

E.D. Sokol, *The Revolt of 1916 in Russian Central Asia* (Baltimore, Md., 1954).

Peter S.H. Tang, *Russian and Soviet Policy in Manchuria and Outer Mongolia, 1911-1913* (Durham, N.C., 1959).

Armnius Vambery, *The Coming Struggle for India* (London, 1885).

Francis Watson, *Frontiers of China* (London, 1966).

Ken Shen Weigh, *Russo-Chinese Diplomacy* (Shanghai, 1928).

Geoffrey Wheeler, *The Modern History of Soviet Central Asia* (London, 1964).

Allen S. Whiting and Sheng Shi-ts'ai, *Sinkiang: Pawn or Pivot* (East Lansing, Mich., 1958).

Arnold T. Wilson, *The Persian Gulf* (London, 1928).

Aitchen K. Wu, *Turkistan Tumult* (London, 1940).

——, *China and the Soviet Union: A Study of Sino-Soviet Relations* (London, 1950).

S. Kuno Yoshi, *Japanese Expansion on the Asiatic Continent* (Berkeley, 1940).

Francis Younghusband, *India and Tibet: A History of Relations which have Subsisted between the Two Countries from the Time of Warren Hastings to 1910* (London, 1910).

S.A. Zenkovsky, *Pan-Turkism and Islam in Russia* (Cambridge, Mass., 1960).

Index